Enlivening
Secondary History

Enlivening Secondary History

40 Classroom Activities for Teachers and Pupils

Peter Davies, Rhys Davies and Derek Lynch

RoutledgeFalmer
Taylor & Francis Group

LONDON AND NEW YORK

First published 2003
by RoutledgeFalmer
11 New Fetter Lane, London EC4P 4EE

Simultaneously published in the USA and Canada
by Routledge
29 West 35th Street, New York, NY 10001

RoutledgeFalmer is an imprint of the Taylor & Francis Group

© 2003 Peter Davies, Derek Lynch and Rhys Davies

Typeset in Gill Sans by
M Rules
Printed and bound in Great Britain by
TJ International, Padstow, Cornwall

British Library Cataloguing in Publication Data
A catalogue record for this book is available from the British Library

Library of Congress Cataloging in Publication Data
A catalog record for this book has been requested

ISBN 0–415–25349–7

CONTENTS

ACKNOWLEDGEMENTS

We would like to thank the HEFCE-funded History 2000 scheme for the generous grant that funded this project in its original form. Our sincere gratitude goes to Paul Hyland, Alan Booth, and Nicky Wilson – the coordinators of the History 2000 initiative – for their support, advice and encouragement. Our grateful thanks also go to the learners and teachers who helped us think through the classroom methods included in this book, and to Anna Clarkson and Louise Mellor at Routledge-Falmer for all their help and guidance. Finally, we would like to acknowledge the input of Yvonne Sinclair, Senior Lecturer in Education at the Institute of Education, Manchester Metropolitan University, Jacqueline Scholes, Head of Art at Tytherington County High School, Macclesfield, John Curtis, Keith Donaldson and Peter Morgan at Longcroft School, Beverley, and Roy Fisher, Philip Woodfine and Janet Conneely at the University of Huddersfield.

The authors are grateful to the following for permission to reproduce material in this book:

Qualifications and Curriculum Authority for material from *Extended Writing in Key Stage 3 History*, 1997.

Raphail F. Scharf for photographs by Willy Georg from *In the Warsaw Ghetto Summer 1941*, published by Robert Hale, London, 1993.

Mansell Virgole Timepix for the *Victorian Family at Home* image.

John Murray (Publishers) Ltd for material from *Britain 1950–1900*, Sheppard and Brown and *Success in 20th Century World Affairs*, Jack Watson.

Haynes and Sutton Publishing for material from *Modern China*, J.A.G. Roberts.

Manchester University Press for material from *The Rise of the Nazis*, C. Fischer, 1995.

Cambridge University Press and the authors for material from *Stalinist Terror*, J. Arch Getty and R.T. Manning, 1994, © Cambridge University Press.

Pearson Education Ltd for material from *The Tudor Parliaments*, M. Graves and *The Hitler State*, M. Broszat.

Boydell and Brewer Ltd for material from *The English and the Norman Conquest*, A. Williams, 1997.

Deutscher Taschenbuch Verlag for material from *Der Erste Weltkrieg 1914–1918*, Gerd Hardach, © Deutscher Taschenbuch Verlag, Munich, Germany (English edition, *The First World War 1914–1918* © 1977 Penguin Books Ltd).

Reed Educational and Professional Publishing for material from *Cold War to Détente*, C. Brown and P. Mooney, 1978.

Berg Publishers for material from *The Great War and the French People*.

The Historical Association and C. M. Riley for material from *The Evidential Understanding, Period Knowledge and the Development of Literacy* in Issue 97 of *Teaching History*.

Dover Publications for material from *Visual illusions: their causes, characteristics and applications*, M. Luckiesh, 1965.

The Publishers have made every effort to contact the copyright holders of material reproduced in this book, but this has not been possible in every case. We would welcome correspondence from individuals or companies that we have been unable to trace.

INTRODUCTION

This book aims to provide History teachers with a 'menu' of possible teaching methods for use in the small-group context. However, it does not aim to be prescriptive or didactic; it is, at bottom, a resource for teachers who like to vary their approach to small-group classes and who would like to experiment more. The resource was produced in its original form under the aegis of the History 2000 project, whose guiding principle – 'Developing Teaching and Learning' – has inspired a plethora of practical educational initiatives, not just this one. It is also important to state that the authors of this book – all practising teachers – have a powerful commitment to enhancing the quality of small-group teaching and learning.

The key idea behind the book is, indeed, a practical one: namely, that teachers can often find themselves short of workable classroom activities, and that a clear, user-friendly manual or guidebook of worked-through teaching strategies could be an extremely useful aid. However, in emphasising the 'hands-on' nature of the project, we should also say that the book as a whole, and many of the specific ideas contained within it, are fully informed by current thinking on teaching and learning.

The context in which this book has emerged is significant. With expanding class sizes a reality, and with new models of learning emerging all the time – for example, Gardner's 'Multiple Intelligence' theory which builds on neurolinguistic programming and explores three types of learning: visual, auditory and kin-esthetic[1] – the time would seem to be right for an exploration of 'active learning', and, in particular, how active learning can be translated into the arena of History teaching at secondary level.

Underpinning this book is the assumption that there is a 'problem': namely, the lack of real variety in the way that small-group classroom sessions are formatted. The 'solution', this book argues, lies in making teaching and learning sessions more interesting, interactive, imaginative and challenging. Peter Frederick has elucidated this situation in the most vivid of terms:

> The highest challenge we face as classroom teachers is to motivate our pupils to love history as we do, and to be joyously involved with the texts, themes, issues, and questions that interest and excite us. Although our

---

1 See, for example, H. Gardner, *The Unschooled Mind: How Children Think and How Schools should Teach*, New York, Basic Books, 1991; H. Gardner, *Frames of Mind: The Theory of Multiple Intelligences*, London, Montana Publishers, 1993; H. Gardner, *Multiple Intelligences: The Theory in Practice*, New York, Basic Books, 1993.

pupils may seem less well motivated or prepared these days, ultimately the responsibility for their motivation rests with us.[2]

Frederick's view has acted as an inspiration to us as we have researched this book. In particular we have come to believe that the onus is on teachers to foster interaction, understanding and, therefore, learning. We also believe strongly in variety and activity in the classroom context. Frederick goes on to state:

> Every study of effective educational practices in recent years cites active and small-group cooperative learning, high expectations combined with frequent feedback, 'hands-on' experiences practising the skills of the discipline and caring teachers as key elements in motivating pupils to learn.[3]

This, again, ties in neatly with the guiding rationale behind this book. Groupwork – in the form of 'buzz group' activity – is fundamental to almost every strategy outlined in this volume. At times whole-group discussion is desirable; at other times it is necessary to split up the 'big' group into a collection of 'mini-groups'. As Petty has argued, individuals generally enjoy any kind of groupwork, 'so long as the teacher is able to direct activities meaningfully.'[4]

This book has also been based on the assumption that pupils learn in different ways: via reading, writing, drawing, and even acting. This is active learning in action. As such, we believe that classroom activities should always incorporate a mix of these elements. Kolb's 'Experiential Learning Theory' is relevant here. As Wright states: 'For learning to be complete, Kolb believes that an individual must first have a concrete experience and then reflect on that experience in an attempt to find meaning. The learner draws conclusions (which is known as abstract conceptualisation) through reflection and discourse and finally enters a phase of active experimentation where ideas and conclusions are tested. This ultimately leads to new experiences and the cycle continues.'[5] Naturally, we hope that the 40 activities presented in this book will provide pupils – and their teachers – with valuable 'concrete experience' upon which to base reflection and experimentation.

The four learning spheres that have been identified in this book – Visuals, Numerical Data, Concepts and Primary Texts – have something in common: they are all important areas of interest for the historian and they all pose a challenge for the imaginative teacher. In addition, it would be fair to say that there is a dearth of practical ideas for teachers interested in varying their approach in these sectors – especially in codified form.

It could be argued that visuals are, perhaps, an under-used type of classroom resource. The contention of Chapter 1 is that visual imagery in history has unlimited potential – particularly if teachers feel confident enough to experiment with:

---

2 P. Frederick, 'Motivating Students by Active Learning in the History Classroom', *Perspectives*, October 1993.

3 *Ibid.*

4 G. Petty, *Teaching Today: A Practical Guide*, Cheltenham, Stanley Thornes, 1993, pp. 221–9.

5 T. Wright, *Educational Policy Studies*, University of Alberta, <http://www.ualberta.ca/~tswright>. Refer to D. Kolb, *The Process of Experiential Learning*, New Jersey, Prentice-Hall, 1984.

(a) a range of techniques designed to get the best out of pictorial sources; and (b) a collection of strategies that involve pupils expressing their own ideas in visual terms (pictorial representation).

In Chapter 2 numerical data comes under the spotlight. Traditionally, if children (and teachers!) are turned off by anything, it is numbers – particularly if they are presented in tabular form (electoral figures, economic data, demographic information etc). So, this section goes on the offensive. How can data be made more interesting? How can teachers make tables of numbers more accessible? The answer comes in the form of puzzles and games, and in 'translating' data into other forms.

Concepts can also intimidate pupils. Maybe they feel more comfortable with 'concrete' things, such as dates, events and people. This again is a challenge: how can such concepts as 'religion', 'feudalism' and 'socialism' be made accessible? Chapter 3 offers some provocative thoughts on this matter. Again, it is a case of being imaginative and, in addition, of not being afraid to 'externalise' ideas.

Chapter 4, for its part, explores what many History teachers would consider to be their 'meat and drink' – primary texts. Here we are talking about speeches, charters and other types of historical document. This section attempts to get away from the 'standard' approach to texts – and moves into some fascinating areas. It explains how pupils can roleplay a document, how over-complex texts can be simplified and, in general terms, how source-based learning can be made much more interesting.

The activities are, therefore, grouped together in four areas. At the same time, however, it is possible to categorise the strategies by genre. For example, in each of the four chapters, there are roleplay-based activities. What follows is neither a scientific nor an exhaustive guide to genres, but it may be an additional aid to the reader:

Type of activity/'genre'		*Activity*
a)	Card-based	2, 32, 37
b)	Hypothesis-based	16, 19, 27, 39
c)	Pictorial representation/ some design or visual element	1–3, 5, 7–11, 15, 20, 25, 26, 28, 30, 34, 35, 40
d)	Annotation	10, 17, 36
e)	Image analysis	4, 23
f)	Puzzle	12
g)	Question-and-answer	6, 32, 33
h)	Roleplay	6, 14, 18, 22, 29, 31, 33, 38
i)	Text analysis	2, 31–38, 40
j)	Worksheet-based	13, 24

It could be said, therefore, that the genres on the left equate to the main themes that underpin the book.

Each of the four chapters has roughly the same structure: ten methods introduced, outlined and examined. In preparing the four sections we went through a set process: designing the teaching methods (with help from colleagues, interviewees and the existing literature), testing them (in the classroom or focus-group environment) and, finally, evaluating their strengths and weaknesses (in tandem with pupils and staff observers). Throughout, the general feeling of both the researchers and the participants was that the 'partnership' between staff and pupils was a positive and beneficial development, and should be encouraged in all spheres of development work.

During the testing of the teaching methods two important issues emerged. First – small groups. Many of the activities included in this book incorporate an element of sub-group or mini-group work (e.g., when a 'big' group of, say, 15 pupils is split up into five groups of three). This strategy has become standard practice for many teachers because their feeling, and that of pupils, is that small-group activity can be more productive than big-group work. A number of general questions are, however, raised by this tactic: (1) What is the ideal size of a 'mini-group': two, three, four or five? When is a group too small and when does it become so big that logistical problems arise? (2) What should be the gender mix of the small groups? (3) Should the groups have a 'fixed' or 'random' membership? (4) Should the teacher circulate between the groups or should he/she leave the mini-groups to it (and maybe even leave the room in an effort to create the most conducive atmosphere for discussion)? (5) Should small-group work totally replace big-group activity? If not, what is the ideal balance? Needless to say, there are no 'right' answers to these questions, but teachers – and pupils – need to show awareness of these issues in specific groupwork situations.

Second – competition. Many of the activities, quite intentionally, contain an element of competition. In a typical class groups may be asked to fulfil a certain task, such as predicting a range of figures in a table, and some kind of inter-group rivalry inevitably ensues. In such a situation the purpose of the competition is not to create antagonisms between class members, but to act as a catalyst for meaningful discussion and, thereby, to enhance learning. For the most part during the 'testing' phase, classroom strategies based on competition worked well and did not attract criticism. Occasionally though, the educational merits of pitting one team of group members against another was questioned. Here the general consensus seemed to be that competition could be, and was usually, a good thing, but that competition should never mean individuals competing against other individuals; in effect, it should always remain group-against-group and should never be allowed to put (perhaps nervous) individuals on the spot. Again, this is an issue that should concern teachers wishing to experiment with different ways of teaching and learning.

This book is aimed at History teachers in the secondary and further education (FE) sectors. We feel that all the strategies and suggestions outlined are relevant and appropriate to teaching and learning in this sphere. The practical ideas are designed for pupils in the 11–18 age range – appropriate to their skills, abilities and interests. We have also ensured that the exemplars utilised in the 40 activity write-ups are fully consonant with Key Stage 3, GCSE, AS- and A-Level syllabi. Thus, subject examples come from a range of historical periods: Britain 1066–1500, 1500–1750 and 1750–1970 and Europe and the World before and after 1900.

Teachers will, therefore, be familiar with most of the subject matter across the 40 activities. The exemplars cover political, social and economic history. We could only really include two or three exemplars in each activity write-up, but obviously each and every technique has numerous applications. Thus, just because we insert a British medieval exemplar into one activity 'spec' does not mean, of course, that this activity can be employed only in classes on British medieval history. Quite the contrary in fact. What we are saying essentially is that teachers can mix and match exemplars and activities as much as they want!

Before proceeding, two caveats are in order. First, these classroom exercises are not to be seen as models of 'best practice', inherently superior to other approaches. Indeed, they can be altered, modified or customised; also, they can be made more complex or, in some cases, simplified, to meet the requirements of a given teacher or course. It is the principle that matters at this stage. Second, we have done a considerable amount of monitoring and we have used classroom feedback to help us assess the impact of each exercise.

There are other features of the book that require highlighting. There is something innately practical and task-based about the classroom strategies explained and outlined. The philosophy that runs throughout this book is simple: passive classes breed passive minds; active classes breed active minds. When pupils 'do things' in the classroom they are provoked, stimulated and enfranchised. It might sound silly, but they also 'remember' practical sessions in the way that they don't necessarily remember teacher-led dictation sessions. This is significant.

It must also be emphasised that, together, the 40 practical activities highlight and foster a range of common and transferable skills. From making a presentation and working as part of a team to analysing texts and assessing visual evidence, these strategies will all help pupils develop as flexible and independent learners. In addition, our experience is that less able individuals relish the kind of practical challenges implicit in these activities as much as, or more than, brighter individuals. In this sense, we feel that the 40 techniques included in this collection will enable teachers to 'add value' to their classes.

Finally, the practical ideas codified in this book are entirely transferable. They could be adapted to suit different academic subjects and different age groups. And on a related note, it must be stressed that teachers are, obviously, free to customise the activities as they wish. 'Timings', 'props' and other details can all be amended and varied in line with specific circumstances and requirements. We think that it would be useful for teachers to be aware of all these points.

In conclusion, we believe that the activities presented and explained in this book will enhance learning in a variety of ways. We believe that meaningful and improved classroom debate can be catalysed. Experimentation, variety, activity, interaction – these are the themes that dominate the book. We hope that teachers will find this book to be a useful, but also a provocative, resource.

Peter Davies, Rhys Davies, Derek Lynch

September 2002

HOW TO USE THE BOOK

We have tried to make the book as clear and easy to use as possible. Each chapter explores one specific area of learning in the subject sphere of History: namely, Visuals, Numerical Data, Concepts, Primary Texts. In each of these sections, 10 teaching methods are introduced, outlined and examined via pro-forma headings which are intended to help the reader move around the book efficiently:

(Activity title)

(The activity in a nutshell)

Description

'Setting and context' – some initial background thoughts

'Learning aims and objectives' – what the activity hopes to achieve

'Resources required' – a quick guide to the 'props' needed

'Breakdown of method in action' – a timed guide to the activity in operation

'Example in action' – a relevant exemplar to consider

'Learning outcomes' – what should come out of the session

Summary

'Merits?' – a quick guide to the benefits and advantages of the activity

'Possible problem/s?' – a quick guide to possible drawbacks

'Finetuning?' – a quick guide to possible improvements and variations.

As regards the methods themselves, it should be noted that some are the equivalent of a one-hour lesson (e.g., they require a 50-minute period to be run effectively), but most are not lessons in themselves; rather, they are short activities designed for, say, a 25-minute or 35-minute slot *within* a lesson. Whatever the time-slot needed, however, all the exercises are self-contained (pre-reading or other preparation would, of course, be helpful).

Each activity is described as being suitable for either Key Stage 3, GCSE or AS/A-Level, and all the classroom strategies are designed to challenge both staff and pupils alike. It is also important to remember that details of activities can be adapted and modified in line with specific teaching requirements and contexts. Teachers who find the book useful can mould the activities further in line with their own thinking. We hope that this book will be a helpful practical aid: clear, user-friendly and full of effective and imaginative teaching ideas.

Further reading

At the end of each chapter we list a number of books and articles that may be of interest to teachers interested in the type of classroom activity covered by that chapter. Here we present a selection of literature that may be of general interest to the imaginative History teacher.

Background and groupwork

D. Anderson, S. Brown and P. Race, (eds), *500 Tips for Further and Continuing Education Lecturers*, London, Kogan Page, 1998.

R. Ashby and P. Lee, 'Discussing the Evidence', *Teaching History*, June 1987.

K. Brzezicki, 'Talking about History: Group Work in the Classroom – Practice and Implications', *Teaching History*, July 1991.

K. Butler, *Learning and Teaching Style in Theory and Practice*, Columbia US, The Learners Dimension, 1984.

J. Cairns, 'Some Reflections on Empathy in History', *Teaching History*, April 1989.

P. Davies, *70 Activities for Tutor Groups*, Aldershot, Gower, 1999.

C. Dickinson, *Effective Learning Activities*, Network Educational Press.

Extended Writing in Key Stage 3 History, London, School Curriculum and Assessment Authority, 1997.

J. Fines, 'Educational Objectives for History – Ten Years On', *Teaching History*, June 1981.

H. Gardner, *The Unschooled Mind: How Children Think and How Schools should Teach*, New York, Basic Books, 1991.

H. Gardner, *Frames of Mind: The Theory of Multiple Intelligences*, London, Montana Publishers, 1993.

H. Gardner, *Multiple Intelligences: The Theory in Practice*, New York, Basic Books, 1993.

G. Gibbs, *Discussion with More Students*, Oxford, Oxford Centre for Staff Development, 1992.

G. Gibbs and T. Habeshaw, *253 Ideas for Your Teaching*, Worcester, Technical and Educational Services, 1990.

P. Gray, 'Problem Solving in History', *Teaching History*, April 1988.

S. Habeshaw, G. Gibbs and T. Habeshaw, *53 Problems with Large Classes*, Bristol, Technical and Educational Services, 1992.

J. Hagerty and M. Hill, 'History and Less Able Children', *Teaching History*, June 1981.

P. Harnett and L. Newman, 'In Touch with the Past: Music Making and Historical Re-enactments', *Teaching History*, February 1998.

J. Hull, 'Practical Points on Teaching History to Less-Able Secondary Pupils', *Teaching History*, October 1980.

D. Jacques, *Small Group Teaching*, SCED Paper 57, 1990.

J. Jenkins and P. Brickley, 'Reflections on the Empathy Debate', *Teaching History*, April 1989.

K. Jenkins and P. Brickley, 'A Level History: On Historical Facts and Other Problems', *Teaching History*, July 1988.

J. King, J. Cox and S. Dymoke, 'The Big Push: Active Learning in the Humanities with Third Year Pupils', *Teaching History*, April 1988.

D. Kolb, *The Process of Experiential Learning*, New Jersey, Prentice-Hall, 1984.

J. Lawrie, 'Desperate Remedies – Inventive Resourcing for the History Classroom', *Teaching History*, October 1994.

V. Little, 'What is Historical Imagination?', *Teaching History*, June 1983.

A. Low-Beer, 'Empathy and History', *Teaching History*, October 1989.

T. May and S. Williams, 'Empathy – A Case of Apathy?' *Teaching History*, October 1987.

B.K. Mbenga, 'Skilful Questioning as an Effective Tool of History Teaching', *Teaching History*, April 1993.

R. Medley, 'Teaching and Learning an Understanding of the Concept of Cause in History', *Teaching History*, April 1988.

W. Oppenheim, 'Complex Games and Simulations in Schools', *Teaching History*, October 1982.

R. Powell, *Active Whole Class Teaching*, Stafford, Robert Powell Publications, 1997.

M. Reynolds, *Groupwork in Education and Training: Ideas in Practice*, London, Kogan Page, 1994.

A. Smith, *Accelerated Learning in Practice*, Stafford, Network Educational Press, 1998.

C. Taylor and J. Allmark, 'A Castle in a Classroom', *Teaching History*, February 1980.

F. Thompson, 'Empathy: An Aim and a Skill to be Developed', *Teaching History*, October 1983.

R.G. Tiberius, *Small-Group Teaching: A Trouble-Shooting Guide*, London, Kogan Page, 1999.

B. Williamson, 'Talking History', *Teaching History*, October 1985.

S. Wood, 'Interpreting Writing Tasks in History Lessons', *Teaching History*, October 1996.

http://www.ualberta./ca/~tswright Tarah Wright, Educational Policy Studies, University of Alberta.

Roleplay

I. Cardall, 'Simulation and History: What Actually Happens in a Classroom?', *Teaching History*, October 1985.

R. Duff, 'Appeasement Roleplay. The Alternative to Munich', *Teaching History*, February 1998.

K. Fleming, 'A Land Fit for Heroes: Recreating the Past through Drama', *Teaching History*, July 1992.

D.L. Ghere, '"You are a Member of the United Nations Commission …" Recent World Crises Simulations', *Teaching History*, June 2001.

P. Goalen, 'The Development of Children's Historical Thinking through Drama', *Teaching History*, April 1996.

P. Goalen and L. Hendy, 'The Challenge of Drama', *Teaching History*, October 1992.

K. Jones, *Simulations: A Handbook for Teachers and Trainers*, London, Kogan Page, 1995.

G. King, J. Tucker and M. Tucker, 'Assessing Drama in GCSE History', *Teaching History*, October 1987.

R. Lee and R. Davis, 'On Monday I took back the Armour and the Videos', *Teaching History*, October 1984.

G. Lyon, 'Reflecting on Rights: Teaching Pupils about Pre-1832 British Politics

Using a Realistic Roleplay', *Teaching History*, June 2001.

I. Luff, '"I've been in the Reichstag": Rethinking Roleplay', *Teaching History*, August 2000.

J. Simkin, 'Practical Problems of Teaching the New History', *Teaching History*, June 1983.

J. Somers, 'Time Capsule: A Fusion of Drama and History', *Teaching History*, July 1991.

E. Towill, 'The Constructive Use of Role Play at Key Stage 3', *Teaching History*, January 1997.

J.R.S. Whiting, 'Report: A Simulation Game Based on Archive Material', *Teaching History*, June 1980.

T.F. Willer and B.M. Haight, 'Indian Village: A Simulation Exercise', *Teaching History*, February 1980.

J. Woodhouse and V. Wilson, 'Celebrating the Solstice: A "History through Drama" Teaching Project on the Iron Age', *Teaching History*, April 1988.

Sources for teachers

Each of the 40 activities presented in the book is accompanied by a series of exemplars. These exemplars are often based around primary texts and we have included a selection of documents where this is so. However, by their very nature, the exemplars can cover only a selection of Key Stage 3, GCSE and AS/A-Level topic areas. Thus, for teachers' convenience we list here a range of primary-source collections that contain a rich array of documents related to Key Stage 3, GCSE and AS/Level topic areas:

Books

P. Adelman, *Victorian Politics*, London, Longman, 1970.

M. Bennett, *The English Civil War*, London, Longman, 2002.

R. Brown, *Revolution, Radicalism and Reform: England 1780–1846*, Cambridge, CUP, 2000.

D.R. Cook, *Lancastrians and Yorkists: The Wars of the Roses*, London, Longman, 1984.

C. Counsell and C. Steer, *Industrial Britain*, Cambridge, CUP, 1993.

L.W. Cowie, *Documents and Descriptions in European History 1714–1815*, London, OUP, 1967.

I. Dawson, *Crime and Punishment through Time*, London, John Murray, 1999.

I. Dawson and I. Coulson, *Medicine and Health through Time* (GCSE), London, John Murray, 1996.

S. Edmonds, *Native Peoples of North America*, Cambridge, CUP, 1993.

E.J. Evans, *Britain before the Reform Act*, London, Longman, 1989.

R. Field, *African Peoples of the Americas*, Cambridge, CUP, 1995.

P. Grey and R. Little, *Germany 1918–1945*, Cambridge, CUP, 1997.

R. Griffin (ed.), *Fascism*, Oxford, OUP, 1995.

A. Harmsworth, *Elizabethan England*, London, John Murray, 1999.

D. Hibberd, *The First World War*, London, Macmillan, 1990.

C. Husbands, *Changing Britain*, Cambridge, CUP, 1992.

P. Ingram, *Russia and the USSR 1905–1991*, Cambridge, CUP, 1997.

A. Johnston, *Protestant Reformation in Europe*, London, Longman, 2002.

P. Jones, *The 1848 Revolutions*, London, Longman, 1981.

S. Lang, *The Twentieth Century World*, Cambridge, CUP, 1998.

G. Martel, *The Origins of the First World War*, London, Longman, 1996.

J. Martell, *A History of Britain from 1967*, London, Nelson, 1988.

D. Martin, *Britain 1815–51*, London, John Murray, 2000.

D. Martin and C. Shephard, *The American West: The Struggle for the Plains 1840–1895*, London, John Murray, 1998.

M. McCauley, *The Origins of the Cold War*, London, Longman, 1987.

M. McCauley, *Stalin and Stalinism*, London, Longman, 1987.

F. McDonough, *Conflict, Communism and Fascism: Europe 1890–1945*, Cambridge, CUP, 2001.

B.R. Mitchell, *Abstract of British Historical Statistics*, Cambridge, CUP, 1962.

R. Overy, *The Origins of the Second World War*, London, Longman, 1998.

M.D. Palmer, *Henry VIII*, London, Longman, 1971.

I. Porter and I.D. Armour, *Imperial Germany 1890–1918*, London, Longman, 1991.

E. Royle, *Chartism*, London, Longman, 1986.

W.J. Sheils, *The English Reformation 1530–1570*, London, Longman, 1989.

C. Shephard, M. Corbishley, A. Large and R. Tames, *The Schools History Project: Contrasts and Connections* (Year 7), London, John Murray, 1991.

C. Shephard, C. Hinton, J. Hite and T. Lomas, *Societies in Change* (Year 8), London, John Murray, 1992.

C. Shephard, A. Reid and K. Shephard, *Peace and War* (Year 9), London, John Murray, 1993.

P. Shuter and T. Lewis, *Skills in History: Book 3 – The Twentieth Century*, London, Heinemann, 1988.

J. Simkin, *Medieval Realms Resource Book*, Brighton, Spartacus Educational, 1991.

J. Whittam, *Fascist Italy*, MUP, Manchester, 1995.

D.G. Williamson, *The Third Reich*, London, Longman, 1982.

A. Wood, *The Russian Revolution*, London, Longman, 1980.

D.G. Wright, *Democracy and Reform 1815–1885*, London, Longman, 1970.

D.G. Wright, *Revolution and Terror in France*, London, Longman, 1974.

D.G. Wright, *Napoleon and Europe*, London, Longman, 1995.

Websites

The Nikzor Holocaust site: an anti-Nazi educational resource devoted to the Holocaust, containing biographies, articles, glossaries and images that could be useful at various stages in the curriculum, especially in areas connected with Nazism and World War II. Go to<http://www.nizkor.org/>.

Channel 4 Learning – a catalogue of audiovisual resources that covers such topics as Race in the Twentieth Century. Details at >http://www.4learning.co.uk/secondary.index.cfm?subjectID+2>.

Greenhead College Norman/Medieval History Links: specifically geared to schools; includes links to sites offering glossaries. Go to <http:www.greenhead.ac.uk.beacon.history.normans.htm>.

American West Trading Post Site (2001): Links to summary histories, images and web pages, including some devoted to Native American tribes. Go to <http://www.americanwest.com/>.

Internet Modern History Sourcebook. Go to <http://www.fordham.edu/halsall.mod.modsbook.html>.

The Avalon Project (Yale Law School): historical documents classified by theme or by period. A useful resource for almost all history courses. Go to <http://www.yale,edu/lawweb/.avalon/avalon.htm>.

George Welling (1997, 2001) The American Revolution – an HTML project: 'From Revolution to Reconstruction' <http://odur.let.rug.nl/~usa/>. Useful for American history components of the syllabus.

Visuals

Picturing the past

Be not afraid of growing slowly.

Be afraid only of standing still.

Chinese proverb

Introduction

We live in a world where young people get most of their knowledge from screens, not pages. Thus, the use of visuals in the teaching of History has huge potential – it can help pupils make sense of the subject and 'visualise' complex ideas. Recent cognitive research also points to the fact that for some learners, a 'visual–spatial' approach to learning is not just beneficial, but vitally necessary if optimum under-standing is to take place.[1] In the secondary sector, the use of visual stimuli can be extremely helpful, especially for the lower-attaining pupil, for whom such terms as 'socialism', 'feudalism' and 'democracy' can be both incomprehensible and alien. So, to 'see' such terms, and to 'see' how they translate into everyday life, can be of huge benefit to pupils, and teachers, in the quest to unravel the conceptual difficul-ties inherent in the subject. This is not to say, however, that the activities outlined in this chapter are not relevant to the more 'academic' or older pupil; the truth is that 'visuals' can help all individuals learn, regardless of age or ability.

Using visuals to 'see' abstract concepts and ideas is one of two general approaches considered by this chapter: 'Draw a Concept' (No. 7) gives pupils the opportunity to visualise and discuss complicated abstract concepts; 'Charts and Diagrams' (No. 3) helps individuals to visualise historical concepts such as 'causation', 'conse-quence', 'change' and 'effect'; and 'Devise a Board Game' (No. 9) looks at how events and political, social and economic phenomena can be charted and repre-sented in a visual form. The other general approach to the use of visuals involves scrutinising and analysing visual images as a way of developing understanding, discussion and debate. Visual sources are invaluable for the clues they provide

---

1 See, for example, H. Gardner, *The Unschooled Mind: How Children Think and How Schools should Teach*, New York, Basic Books, 1991; H. Gardner, *Frames of Mind: The Theory of Multiple Intelligences*, London, Montana Publishers, 1993; H. Gardner, *Multiple Intelligences: The Theory in Practice*, New York, Basic Books, 1993.

about the past, and historians are blessed with a deep pool of sources from which to draw. However, as teachers, how effectively do we use visual images in our teaching as a way of unlocking the past? Do we encourage our pupils to scrutinise visual sources and use them as effectively as they can? Or do cartoons, photographs, propaganda posters and portraits receive only a superficial glance and maybe a few off-the-cuff comments? In an effort to make more of sources, we present: 'Freeze Frame' (No. 6), which allows pupils to empathise with characters in a visual via roleplay; 'Introductory Images' (No. 4), which provokes and challenges them via graphic images; and 'Annotation' (No. 10), which encourages young people to dissect a visual source in detail. For all the examples, it must be stressed that the quality of the artwork is incidental; visual images are produced and utilised in order to enhance discussion and learning and therefore maximise the learner's understanding of the subject.

Activities

1 Propaganda Posters (GCSE)

2 Convert a Text (Key Stage 3)

3 Charts and Diagrams (Key Stage 3)

4 Introductory Images (Key Stage 3)

5 Class Craft (Key Stage 3, GCSE and AS/A-Level)

6 Freeze Frame (GCSE)

7 Draw a Concept (AS/A-Level)

8 Coloured History (GCSE)

9 Devise a Board Game (Key Stage 3)

10 Annotation (Key Stage 3)

The most suitable level for usage is indicated in brackets. However, it should be noted that, with a little adaptation and customisation, many activity ideas contained within this chapter could also be employed at other levels.

ACTIVITY 1

Propaganda Posters

DIY totalitarianism in action

Description

Setting and Context

This is a particularly useful activity for analysing the doctrine of a political or social movement, or assessing the mood of a particular audience from the past. Posters can be devised after looking at a number of written sources which outline the ideas of an organisation, whether in the form of speeches, radio broadcasts or news sheets. In the example given, participants are asked to devise a Nazi propaganda poster after analysing a range of written sources dealing with the party's programme and the movement's appeal to the discontented elements of German society in the early 1930s. The teacher could even 'model' an example first.

Learning aims and objectives

Pupils are to convert Nazi ideas – taken from a selection of written documents – into a visual medium and so enhance their understanding of the main tenets of the party's ideology and the appeal of the movement. The objectives of the exercise are to enable group members to: (1) analyse and discuss (in small groups) a political movement's ideology and appeal to the people; (2) produce a visual image illustrating the appeal of the party to a certain social group – after a period of discussion and analysis of primary sources; (3) develop an empathetic awareness of what it was like (in this case) to produce propaganda in 1930s Germany; (4) present their ideas to the rest of the class and share findings.

Resources required

- [ ] A range of written documentary evidence
- [ ] Sugar/poster paper
- [ ] Coloured marker pens
- [ ] Sellotape or Blu-Tack (to display the posters)

Breakdown of method in action

Time Needed	Phase of Activity
10 mins	The teacher leads a discussion about the appeal of the Nazis to German people in 1933, explains the activity, and places participants in small groups. One group is asked to devise a poster that would appeal to the working classes; another, one to appeal to the middle classes; another, one to appeal to the Junker class; another, one to appeal to German women; and a fifth, a poster that would have cross-sectional appeal.
25 mins	The groups produce their own particular posters.
15 mins	The young people display and present their posters to the class as a whole; class members take notes on the Nazi party's main ideas and how the movement attempted to achieve cross-sectional mass support. The role of the teacher is clearly understood by the participants. They like the way that they are allowed to work by themselves (with the teacher being on hand to assist if necessary). In this way, the task is very pro-active for the pupils involved.

(Total time needed = 50 minutes)

Good exemplars

1 *Germany 1918–1939* (see above)

The following sources can be used as stimulus material to help produce the Nazi propaganda posters:

Source A *A Nazi propaganda pamphlet (1932)*[2]

> Attention! Gravediggers at work!
>   Middle-class citizens! Retailers! Craftsmen! Tradesmen!
>   A new blow aimed at your ruin is being prepared and carried out in Hanover!
>   The present system enables the gigantic concern WOOL-WORTH (America)
>   Supported by finance capital, to build a new vampire business in the centre of the city ... to expose you to complete ruin ...
>   ... Defend yourself, middle-class citizen! Join the mighty organisation that alone is in a position to conquer your arch-enemies. Fight with us in the Section for Craftsmen and Retail Traders within the great freedom movement of Adolf Hitler!
>   Put an end to the system!

2   J. Noakes and G. Pridham, *Nazism 1919–1945 Vol. I: The Rise to Power 1919–1934*, Exeter, University of Exeter Press, 1991, p. 76.

Source B   *From a resolution passed at a Nazi meeting for farmers, January 1928[3]*

> We have recognised that the distress of agriculture is inseparably bound up with the political misery of the German people. Let us do away with this Marxist–capitalist extortion system that has made Germany, our homeland, powerless, without honour, defenceless, and has turned free German farmers into poor, misused slaves of the world stock exchange.

Source C   *A sSpeech made by Hitler on 26 October 1920[4]*

> We need some national pride again … We need a national will. We must not say: We can't do that. We must be able to do it. In order to smash this disgraceful peace treaty, we must regard every means as justified … We must have blind faith in our future, in our recovery … (Youth of Germany) your place is with us, with the people. You are still young and still have the fire of enthusiasm in your veins, come over to us, join our fighting party!

Source D   *Hitler speaking in 1934 at the Reich Party Conference[5]*

> Woman has her battlefield too: with each child that she brings into the world for the nation she is fighting on behalf of the nation.

2 Russia 1917–1941

Learners could be asked to produce posters encouraging Russian citizens to work as part of Stalin's industrialisation programme of the 1930s. The following sources can be used as stimulus material:

Source A   *Part of a speech Joseph Stalin made to Soviet businessmen in 1931[6]*

> It is sometimes asked whether it is not possible to slow the tempo a bit, to put a check on the movement. No, comrades, it is not possible! The tempo must not be reduced! On the contrary, we must increase it as much as is within our powers and possibilities. To slacken the tempo would mean falling behind. And those who fall behind get beaten. But we do not want to be

---

3   G. Lacey and K. Shephard, *Germany 1918–1945: A Study in Depth*, London, John Murray, 1997, p. 45
4   Noakes and Pridham, *op. cit.*, p. 17.
5   Lacey and Shephard, *op. cit.*, p. 137.
6   D. Heater, *Case Studies in Twentieth Century World History*, London, Longman, 1988, p. 64.

> beaten. No, we refuse to be beaten! ... Do you want our socialist fatherland to be beaten and to lose its independence? If you do not want this you must put an end to its backwardness in the shortest possible time and develop genuine Bolshevik tempo in building up its socialist system of economy. There is no other way. That is why Lenin said during the October Revolution: 'Either perish, or overtake and outstrip the advanced capitalist countries'.

Source B   *From Stalin's Collected Works (1931)*[7]

> We must ... create in our country an industry which would be capable of re-equipping and organising not only the whole of our industry but also our agriculture ... The history of Russia shows ... that because of her backwardness she was constantly being defeated. We are fifty or a hundred years behind the advanced countries. We must make good this distance in ten years. Either we do it or we will go under.

Learning outcomes

At the end of the activity, pupils will be able to: (1) critically analyse the main values of a movement or organisation; (2) translate ideas into a visual form; (3) evaluate a group's appeal to different social constituencies.

Summary

Merits?

- [ ] Inspires pupils to think in more depth about a certain ideology.
- [ ] By asking for posters to be designed for specific audiences, the activity encourages pupils to empathise.
- [ ] Visual images help pupils to remember ideas.
- [ ] By working a set of ideas into one image, individuals are made to focus on the most important tenets of a value-system.
- [ ] Groupwork leads to maximum pupil engagement (the teacher is seen by the young people as a facilitator – managing the learning environment).

Possible problem?

Laziness – pupils who just copy visual images rather then interpreting the written sources. A possible solution could be to ask participants to prepare a brief oral justification, explaining the rationale for their choice of image.

---

7   T. Fiehn, *Russia and the USSR 1905–1941: A Study in Depth*, London, John Murray, 1996, p. 87.

Finetuning?

☐ Stimulus material could be strictly controlled so as to encourage participants to develop their image independently.

☐ An archive of symbols and images could be made available as a prompt to certain participants.

ACTIVITY 2

Convert a Text

Turn one type of source into another

Description

Setting and context

This method can be used as a means of encouraging younger pupils to visualise, and therefore mentally comprehend, a historical event or location – when all they have to go on is the evidence of a written text. The activity could also be used with older pupils as a way of making them think deeper about abstract concepts or a certain idea from, or aspect of, the past.

Learning aims and objectives

To allow class members the opportunity to think deeply about, and visualise, a key concept, event or idea contained within a written document. The objectives of the exercise are to enable pupils to: (1) analyse and discuss documentary evidence; (2) imagine how the event or concept would 'look' in a visual form; (3) translate the written evidence into a visual form by way of a painting, sketch or collage etc; (4) compare and contrast the pupils' visual interpretations of the event/concept with other interpretations, and check for consistency.

Resources required

☐ Written text
☐ Art materials
☐ Paper

Breakdown of method in action:

Time needed	Phase of activity
5 mins	The teacher explains the activity – and so ensures maximum concentration and task-definition.
5 mins	Teacher reads out the written source to the class; pupils then focus on the source, forming a mental picture of it as they do so.
10 mins	In tandem with the class, the teacher establishes the 'facts' as contained in the source. This is the starting point for the activity.

| 20 mins | Individuals produce their own visual representation of the event/concept under consideration (and as contained in the source). |
| 10 mins | The teacher then discusses the images produced with the class, assessing similarities and differences between the images and, if possible, displaying an 'actual' picture of the event/concept. |

(Total time needed = 50 minutes)

Good exemplars

I *The Burning of Latimer and Ridley*[8] *(see Figure Ia)*

Source A   *John Foxe's Book of Martyrs*

> Dr Ridley and Mr Latimer both came to the stake, looking towards heaven. Dr Ridley smiled at Mr Latimer and hugged him. 'Don't be sad brother', said Dr Ridley to Mr Latimer, 'God will help us, I'm sure.'
>
> They both then made their way to the stake, knelt and prayed. Dr Ridley gave small presents to the men who were watching, many of whom were weeping strongly. From these small presents, the spectators would remember this good man. Then the blacksmith took a chain of iron and placed it about their waists and then knocked in the staple.
>
> Dr Ridley's brother brought him a bag of gunpowder and tied it about his neck. His brother did the same to Mr Latimer.
>
> They then brought a lighted faggot and laid it at Dr Ridley's feet. Mr Latimer then turned to Dr Ridley and said 'Be of good cheer Master Ridley, for we shall this day light a candle in England which shall never be put out.'
>
> Mr Latimer cried out 'Father in Heaven, receive my soul' and soon died with seeming little pain. But Dr Ridley, due to the bad arrangement of the fire (the faggots being green and piled so high, that the flames were kept down by the green wood), struggled in much pain until one of the bystanders pulled the faggots with a hook. Where Ridley saw the flame come up, he leaned himself to that side. As soon as the fire touched the gunpowder he was seen to stir no more. The dreadful sight filled almost every eye with tears.

8 *John Foxe's Book of Martyrs*, London, Word, 2000.

Figure 1a The burning of Latimer and Ridley – one pupil's pictorial representation of the text.

2 *The Round City at Baghdad*[9] *(see Figure 1b)*

Source A   *A description of the city of Baghdad*

Pupils read a description of the city of Baghdad and note the following:

☐ The Royal palace and the mosque were in the middle. The palace was placed so that when Muslims prayed towards Mecca they had to bow to the Caliph's palace as well.

---

9   C. Culpin, *Discovering the Past: Y7 Contrasts and Connections*, London, John Murray, 1991.

- [ ] Open spaces surrounded the palace.
- [ ] The palace was protected by circular walls which separated the palace and its grounds from the rest of the city.
- [ ] The city had four main gates. Over each of these gates was a gatehouse. When the Caliph made a speech to the people, he spoke from the roof of the gatehouse. Each gate had a guard of 1000 men.
- [ ] Areas of the city could easily be sealed off in case of riots or other disturbances.
- [ ] The whole of the Round City was surrounded by a dry moat and another wall and a ditch on the outside. Soldiers could be assembled in the moat in times of danger.

On the basis of this, how would pupils represent the Round City at Baghdad in pictorial form?

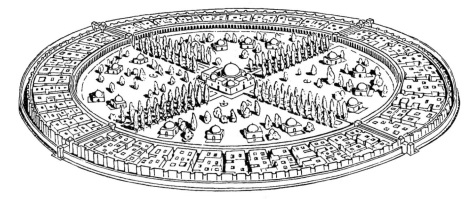

Figure 1b The Round City of Baghdad.

How close to the 'real thing' (above) would the pupils get in their pictorial representations?

3 *The murder of Thomas Becket* (see Figure 1c)

Source A   *From the eyewitness account of Edward Grim, written in the early 1170s[10]*

> The murderers came in full armour with swords and axes. The monks begged the Archbishop to flee to the Cathedral. But he refused. He had wanted to be a martyr (someone who dies for their cause) for a long time. However, the monks seized him and pushed him into the church. The four knights followed. The Archbishop ordered the doors of the cathedral to be kept open.
>
> They tried to drag the Archbishop out of the cathedral. But Thomas clung on to a pillar and would not let go. One of the knights. Reginald Fitzurse, cut him on the top of his head. By the same stroke he almost cut off my arm. For, when the monks

---

10 Kelly, Rees and Shuter, *Living Through History: Medieval Realms*, London, Heinemann, 1997, p. 35.

ran away, I stood by the Archbishop and put my arms round him to protect him. He stood firm to a second blow to the head. At the third blow he fell to his knees, whispering, 'For the name of Jesus and the protection of the Church I am ready to die.' Roger Brito gave him a terrible blow as he lay on the floor. Hugh Mauclerc put his foot on Becket's neck. He scattered blood and brains across the floor shouting to the others 'Let us go. This fellow will not be getting up again'.

On the basis of this, how would pupils represent the murder of Thomas Becket in pictorial form?

Figure 1c The murder of Thomas Becket.

Learning outcomes

On completion of the exercise, pupils will be able to: (1) assess the meaning and significance of a text; (2) visualise a text and, in so doing, explore a variety of important issues and themes; (3) critically analyse the relationship between a text and an image.

Summary

Merits?

- ☐ Encourages participants to think hard about, and constantly revisit, written evidence.
- ☐ Allows pupils to express their own ideas without fear of being 'wrong'. If handled correctly, this exercise can offer teacher and pupils a good opportunity to address the key issue of judging secondary sources for reliability and utility.
- ☐ Young people enjoy comparing their images with those of their peers and, if available, contemporary visuals of the event.
- ☐ The task can be particularly appealing to lower attainers, who might enjoy expressing themselves through 'drawing' rather than 'writing'.

Possible problems?

- ☐ May not be taken seriously by individuals in the post-16 age group. Once again, the teacher may need to 'sell' this activity to pupils.
- ☐ Care must be taken not to present this activity as merely a 'draw a picture' exercise – instead, it is important to discuss the images as a way of developing pupils' understanding of a text and for spotting potential anachronisms which can be identified by comparing their images with the 'real article'.

Finetuning?

- ☐ The introduction of further stimulus material – possibly the use of video? Or would this defeat the whole point of the exercise?

ACTIVITY 3

Charts and Diagrams

Organising ideas – effectively

Description

Setting and context

This is not so much an activity in itself, but rather a means of allowing individuals to organise ideas and concepts in a visual manner. The skill of organising ideas and concepts is central to the work of any historian, but it can be quite challenging for pupils across a range of ages and abilities. The ideas presented below are certainly not new, but are stimulating nonetheless. The recent emphasis on analytical thinking and extended writing in the secondary sector has led to the use of 'sorting devices' – tools that help and encourage group members to think in a questioning way. The novelty is that, for once, pupils are allowed to 'see' historical issues and arguments. Discussion can follow on metacognitive issues – how pupils remember things, whether pictures and charts help, etc.

Learning aims and objectives

To help pupils think clearly and analytically about key historical issues.

Resources required

☐ Blank charts and diagrams
☐ Pens

Breakdown of method in action

Time needed	Phase of activity
10 mins	Teacher introduces exercise.
30 mins	Pupils work, in pairs or individually, on charts and diagrams.
10 mins	Teacher chairs plenary session.

(Total time needed = 50 minutes)

Good exemplars

See Figures 1d–h.[11]

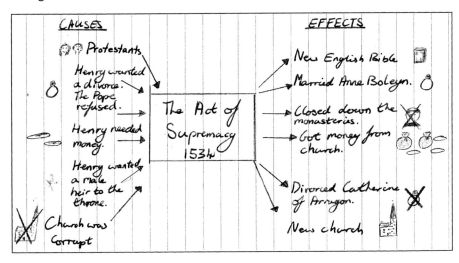

Figure 1d 'Cause and effect' allows pupils to carry out a fairly conventional sorting activity.

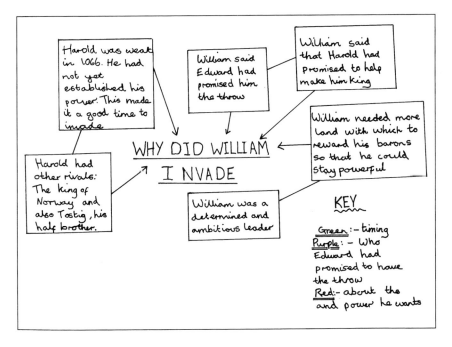

Figure 1e 'Cause and effect' diagrams can also be used to help with the flow of ideas.

---

11 *Extended Writing in Key Stage 3 History*, London, School Curriculum and Assessment Authority, 1997.

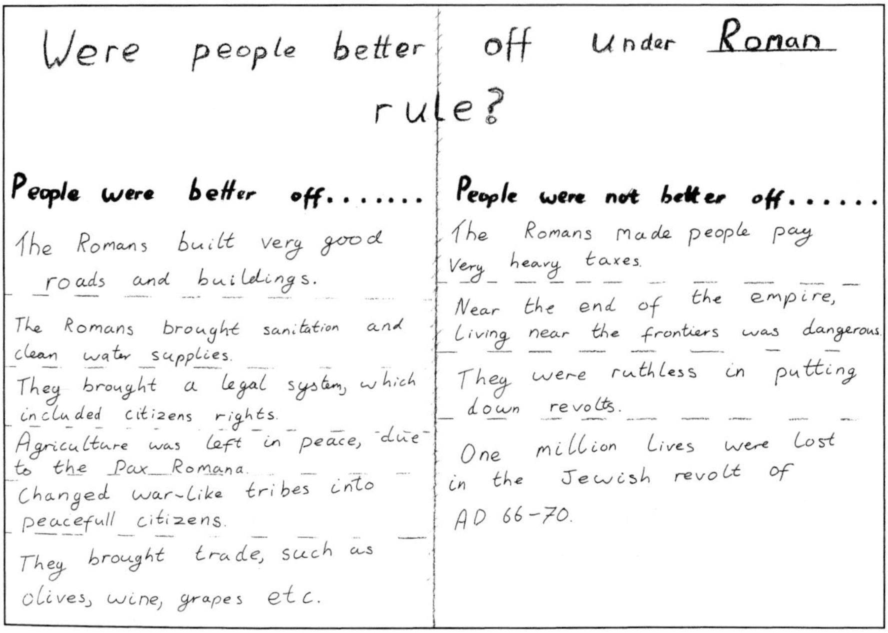

Were people better off Under __Roman__ rule?

People were better off.......	People were not better off......
The Romans built very good roads and buildings.	The Romans made people pay very heavy taxes.
The Romans brought sanitation and clean water supplies.	Near the end of the empire, living near the frontiers was dangerous.
They brought a legal system, which included citizens rights.	They were ruthless in putting down revolts.
Agriculture was left in peace, due to the Pax Romana.	One million lives were lost in the Jewish revolt of AD 66-70.
Changed war-like tribes into peacefull citizens.	
They brought trade, such as olives, wine, grapes etc.	

Figure 1f 'Sorting devices' can be used as preparation for an extended piece of writing where an analysis of historical factors is required.

RESEARCH STUDY GUIDE

THEME   Native People of America: The Indian Tribes

RESEARCH TITLE   Choose one of the following Indian groups for your study

| PLAINS INDIANS | | PUEBLO INDIANS | | WOODLAND INDIANS |

AIM   to produce a study of your chosen Indian group that includes information about these

AREAS OF INVESTIGATION

ENVIRONMENT	**SETTLEMENT**	**MEANS OF PROVIDING FOOD**
Where did they live?	What were their homes like?	Were they farmers?
What was the area they lived in like?	Did they settle in one place?	How did they get their food?
How did this affect the way that they lived?	Did they live in groups or alone?	What did they eat?

INDUSTRY AND TECHNOLOGY	**SOCIAL STRUCTURE**	**BELIEFS AND CULTURE**
What tools were used?	Did they have a leader?	What did they believe?
What materials were used?	How did they make decisions?	How did they worship?
How did they make things?	What role did women play?	What artefacts did they make?

TIME AVAILABLE   you have 4.5 hours to complete your study

WORD LIMIT   600

INCLUDE   title
pictures, diagrams, maps etc .
a bibliography (a list of all the books and other sources)

Figure 1g This 'sorting device' can be used to help plan research.

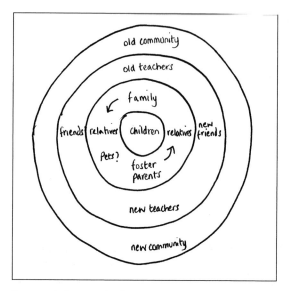

Figure 1h 'Ripple diagrams' give pupils the opportunity to examine the effects of historical events on people's lives. This one illustrates the impact of evacuation during World War II on different groups of people.

Learning outcomes

On completion of the exercise, pupils will be able to: (1) organise and sort historical data into a simple and accessible chart or diagram; (2) plan an essay (or another type of assignment) on the basis of a graphic; (3) critically review the main issues and themes within a historical debate.

Summary

These exercises allow individuals to organise and shape their ideas into an easily understood and highly accessible form. They can be used to good effect with all pupils, from Year 7 to Upper 6th. If they are completed on poster paper and displayed to other class members, these devices can spark excellent discussion and debate.

Merits?

☐ Externalises pupils' ideas.
☐ Clarifies thinking.
☐ Includes a helpful visual element.

Possible problems?

☐ Explaining the exercise in simple terms.

Finetuning?

☐ Get pairs of pupils to double up and compare notes?

ACTIVITY 4

Introductory Images

Dramatise the past

Description

Setting and context

This activity uses the power of visual sources as a means of making pupils aware of the gravity of a particularly harrowing or alarming historical event – or as a way of introducing a topic in an attention-grabbing way, thus providing class members with the 'big picture' before moving on to more in-depth analysis.

Learning aims and objectives

To introduce and encourage young people to think about a dramatic historical episode through a thorough study of visual material. The objectives of the exercise are to enable pupils to: (1) analyse a number of pictorial sources; (2) comprehend a range of visual sources and evaluate and record their feelings towards it; (3) explore their responses in small-group and whole-group contexts; (4) generate a set of provocative questions about the sources that could aid further enquiry.

Resources required

☐ A number of visual images
☐ Pens and paper

Breakdown of method in action

Time needed	Phase of activity
5 mins	Teacher organises the class into small groups and explains the purpose of the exercise. Images are distributed – one to each group. Teacher perhaps models a previously used visual.
25 mins	Each group looks at an image. Discussion follows and the pupils prepare a set of questions about the source. Groups then swap images; the process is repeated until all the images have been analysed.
15 mins	Teacher-led discussion on reactions to the images and the questions that have been prompted by the individual sources.

(Total time needed = 45 minutes)

Good exemplar

1 *The Holocaust* (see Figures 1i–k)[12]

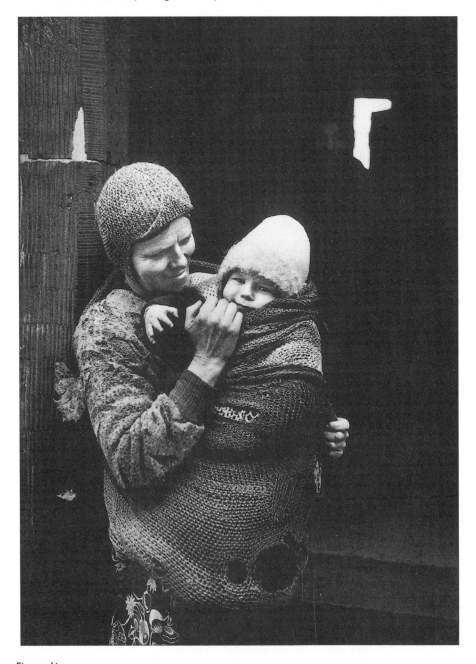

Figure 1i

---

12 R.F. Scharf, *In the Warsaw Ghetto, Summer 1941*, Robert Hale, London, 1993.

Figure 1j

Figure 1k

Learning outcomes

At the end of the activity, individuals will be able to: (1) assess the meaning of a range of images; (2) evaluate their response to the sources in the context of group discussion.

Summary

Merits?

- [ ] The visuals provide class members with the 'big picture' before they are asked to move on to more specific issues.
- [ ] Images are accessible and open to interpretation.
- [ ] Allows pupils to think and reflect for themselves and with one another (particularly important when the images are so sensitive).
- [ ] All class members are actively involved in the learning process, with the teacher taking on the role of facilitator rather than instructor.

Possible problems?

- [ ] Sources need to be carefully selected and the learning environment carefully controlled, particularly with a topic as sensitive as the Holocaust. In this respect, 'softer' images such as a pile of victims' shoes or a mother sheltering her child from the gun of an SS officer can be just as powerful as, say, a graphic image of bulldozed corpses (and do not detract from the gravity of what happened). These not-so-obvious images can also provoke good-quality questions from the pupils and leave them keen to want to know more. As teachers, we must be careful not to play to young people's curiosity about the grotesque, which can lead to overwhelming them with harrowing images.

Finetuning?

- [ ] Introduction of music – how would this affect the impact of the visuals?
- [ ] Show the visuals along with questions to think about and discuss e.g. 'What is happening in this picture?' 'Who are the children?' 'Where are these people being taken to?'

ACTIVITY 5   *Suitable for Key Stage 3, GCSE and AS/A-Level*

Class Craft

Touch, feel and paint the past

Description

Setting and context

This classroom technique emerged from the work of Neil Morley, an MA Art pupil at Staffordshire University. As part of Neil's MA course, he produced a number of images that explored the structure and quirkiness of Britain's class system. He used a wide range of materials, including paints, textiles and icons – and the outcome was a number of collage-type posters. Many historical periods can be explored in this way.

Learning aims and objectives

To allow class members to explore the make-up of societies through the medium of art. The objectives of the exercise are to enable pupils to: (1) discuss class hierarchies and divisions; (2) portray class through various materials and colour; (3) work in groups.

Resources required

- [ ] Various materials including paint, glue and textiles (various fabrics, wallpaper, etc)
- [ ] Photocopied images from History textbooks
- [ ] Newspaper headlines and pictures

Breakdown of method in action

Time needed	Phase of activity
10 mins	Teacher explains exercise, circulates images, and hands out art materials.
30 mins	Pupils work on collages.
10 mins	Teacher displays collages and chairs discussion on main themes to emerge from the session.

(Total time needed = 50 minutes)

Good exemplar

1 *Class systems in Tudor Britain or Pre-Revolutionary Russia represented in collage form* (see Figures 1l, 1m)

Note that newspapers, paint and fabric could be used simply and effectively by pupils to produce collages that demonstrate the main tenets of a variety of different ideologies and political and economic system e.g. Communism versus capitalism; Fascism; Democracy versus Dictatorship; Puritanism; Feudalism etc.

Figure 1l Pupils' work – Tudor and Stuart Britain.

In the collage shown in Figure 1l, materials have been used to good effect to symbolise the three classes of Tudor and Stuart Britain. The denim goes well with the modern newspaper headlines of 'WANT', 'WORK', 'FEAR AND LOATHING' and 'POOR' in portraying the plight of the lower orders. The patterned material, with images of fast cars and yeoman houses, symbolises the middle ranks of merchants and doctors etc, while the velvet and images of royalty and expensive furniture illustrate the luxury and decadence of the rich.

Figure 1m Pupils' work – Russian Revolution.

Lenin leading the oppressed to a bright new world. One can clearly see the symbolism of black and white icons and newspaper photographs representing the lower orders and the colour of Lenin's Utopia.

Learning outcomes

Following the session, participants will be able to: (1) represent social patterns in visual form; (2) critically assess the class make-up of a society.

Summary

Merits?

☐ Everyone feels involved. The use of a full range of materials really brings a potentially dull subject alive.

☐ It enables young people to see something as abstract as the class system in another form (via images, icons and colour). They can actually 'feel' it too (with different textiles and different materials being used to symbolise different social classes).

☐ The use of newspaper headlines in the collages enables participants to make comparisons between the historical period being studied and modern society.

☐ This was, perhaps, a rather 'messy' type of exercise, but the young people involved themselves actively in it. They also worked with confidence, knowing that there were no 'right' or 'wrong' outcomes.

Possible problems?

Time – this is a demanding activity that may need a couple of hours to complete if done properly. Some of the work could be completed as a homework task.

Freeze Frame

Bring alive a picture, photo or painting

Description

Setting and context

This activity allows pupils to empathise with characters from the past, as featured in a visual source. In essence, the exercise involves pupils 'acting out', and then 'freezing', a picture, photograph or cartoon with important historical connotations. And those individuals who are not acting out the key 'visual' roles also take an active part in the session in the sense that they devise and ask questions to those in role. Consequently this activity can be used wherever the teacher wishes to break down a visual source – and study individual characters in detail.

Learning aims and objectives

Pupils are to acquire an empathetic understanding of the characters in a visual source, such as their social class, roles, ideas, aims, ideology, profession and historical context. The objectives of the exercise are to enable individuals to: (1) study one or a number of pictorial sources in detail; (2) ask relevant questions about the characters in the sources; (3) reach an empathetic understanding of the key personalities featured in the sources, including their ideology, role and position in society; (4) improve self-confidence through acting and speaking in class.

Resources required

☐ A range of visual sources
☐ Paper for writing questions

Breakdown of method in action

Time needed	Phase of activity
10 mins	Teacher introduces the aims of the session, distributes the set visual source and chairs a brief discussion about the content, bias and context of the source.
10 mins	The teacher sets up the 'freeze frame' with class members. The pupils take on one of two roles: a few are assigned characters in the visual source to act out; the rest of the class, meanwhile, jot down any questions they would like to ask of the personalities in the source being roleplayed. While

the questions are being devised, the pupils in role think about their characters and how they're 'feeling' in the set visual source. A question-and-answer session ensues between 'audience' and 'cast'.

10 mins	The teacher oversees a whole-class discussion about the learning outcomes to emerge from the exercise.

(Total time needed = 30 minutes)

Good exemplars

1 *Victorian family life* (see Figure 1n)

Figure 1n A Victorian family at home.[13]

---

13 R. Hamer, *Life and Work in 19th Century Britain*, London, Heinemann, 1995.

What questions would pupils ask of the family members in this 'freeze frame'? How would the characters respond?

Possibly:

'Dad – what do you do for a living?'

'Mum – what hopes and fears do you have for your children?'

'Kiddies – can you read and write yet?'

How would the characters respond?

Possibly:

Dad: 'I work in a mill – and I earn very little.'

Mum: 'I hope they will all survive into adulthood – but I fear they won't make it.'

Kiddies: 'No.'

Learning outcomes

On completion of the activity, pupils will be able to: (1) empathise with personalities from the past; (2) assess the motivation and attitude of key characters in a period; (3) critically review the main issues and controversies to come out of a source.

Summary

Merits?

- [ ] Increased participation due to 'fun element'.
- [ ] Encourages deep scrutiny of a visual image, thus enhancing learning and retention.
- [ ] All group members are involved in the session in some way – whether acting out a role or devising questions.

Possible problem?

- [ ] Improvisation can lead to historical inaccuracies.

Finetuning?

- [ ] Actors could use props or name badges so as to eliminate any 'who is who?' confusion.
- [ ] More drama? The scene *pre-still image* could be acted out, as could a possible scene, *post-still image*.

ACTIVITY 7

Draw a Concept

Transpose an idea into an image

Description

Setting and context

As pupils get older, their understanding of the abstract in history improves. Concepts such as 'Socialism', 'Revolution' and 'Fascism' are (normally) more easily understood among individuals over the age of 16 than among younger people. The purpose of this activity is to give pupils an opportunity to think about, visualise, and therefore discuss, a historical concept.

Learning aims and objectives

To make young people think more deeply about a historical concept and, by asking participants to visualise the idea, to promote discussion and debate about the concept in question. The objectives of the exercise are to enable pupils to: (1) develop a visual understanding of a certain idea; (2) acquire an in-depth awareness of an abstract concept; (3) work in groups and therefore share ideas; (4) report back to the class on the conclusions reached during the exercise.

Resources required

☐ Coloured marker pens
☐ Large sheets of paper
☐ Sellotape (for display purposes)

Breakdown of method in action

Time needed	Phase of activity
10 mins	The teacher introduces the activity and leads a preliminary big-group discussion on the set concept (so as to familiarise participants with the main issues surrounding it). Class members are then divided up into groups of three or four and materials are distributed.
20 mins	In small groups, pupils visualise the concept and then represent it in graphic form.

| 20 mins | Individuals feed back their ideas to the rest of the class – and big-group discussion follows. |

(Total time needed = 50 minutes)

Good exemplars

1 *Pilgrimage* (see *Figure 1o*)

How would learners represent the medieval concept of 'Pilgrimage' in graphic form? What ideas and images are associated with the term? Figure 1o incorporates three different responses.

Figure 1o Pilgrimage.

How would individual pupils explain these images? In what ways would they provoke discussion? How does pictorial representation help us understand the idea better? What issues and controversies are raised by the whole exercise?

This activity can be used to promote discussion around a whole range of historical concepts from AS and A Level syllabi: Unification, Revolution, Feudalism, Reformation, Liberty, Equality, Fraternity, Nazism, Marxism etc.

2 Revolution *(see Figure 1p)*

One pupil's effort to represent 'Revolution' in pictorial form is shown in Figure 1p.

Figure 1p Revolution.

How would the pupil explain his or her thinking? How would this image provoke discussion?

3 Reformation *(see Figure 1q)*

One pupil's effort to represent 'Reformation' in pictorial form is shown in Figure 1q.

Figure 1q Reformation.

How would the pupil explain his or her thinking? How would this image provoke discussion?

Learning outcomes

Following the exercise, class members will be able to: (1) analyse an abstract historical concept; (2) represent an idea in visual form; (3) reflect on the meaning and significance of individuals' pictorial representations.

Summary

Merits?

☐ Through a process of visualisation and discussion, this exercise provides class members with the opportunity to develop a clearer and more memorable understanding of an abstract concept.

☐ The exercise gets pupils to think about a key concept is a useful way to finish off a topic.

Possible problems?

☐ Learners' natural tendency to produce 'concrete' images rather than representative pictorial ideas.

☐ Class members' inadequate drawing skills may distort a concept's true meaning.

☐ Follow-up discussion of the images produced is vital to securing understanding. Without this, individuals might feel that their understanding of a concept may be vague or uncertain. The teacher should be available throughout to help clarify pupils' thinking – but care must be taken to avoid influencing the nature and overall meaning of the images.

Finetuning?

☐ Participants to devise a caption to go with the posters as a way of clarifying the message of the image?

☐ The exercise could take place *before* the study of a specific concept takes place – in order to ascertain pupils' prior knowledge and preconceptions of it.

ACTIVITY 8

Coloured History

A provocative exercise in 'what if?'

Description

Setting and context

Can you imagine the patriotic Union Jack in yellow, white and green? An absurd image indeed. But it does raise the issue of colour/image coordination. Thus, the purpose of this activity is to explore the relationship between the use of colour and imagery – particularly with regard to political icons and flags – and also to stimulate discussion about historical symbols and their significance. What often follows is a deeper understanding of not just the impact of colour in historical symbols, but the meaning of the actual symbols in themselves.

Learning aims and objectives

To allow pupils the opportunity to analyse political imagery, particularly with regard to the use of colour and the effect of colour in highlighting a message. The objectives of the exercise are to enable pupils to: (1) experiment with a number of colours in relation to a well known historical symbol; (2) explore the effects of different colours on enhancing or distorting the message implicit in a symbol.

Resources required

☐ Paper
☐ Paints or coloured marker pens

Breakdown of method in action

Time needed	Phase of activity
5 mins	The teacher introduces the activity, sorts individuals into small groups of three or four, and distributes materials. Each group is instructed to colour their symbol/flag in a different way.
15 mins	Each group designs and then colours its symbol/flag.

25 mins	The completed designs are circulated around the class – and each mini-group is invited to jot down a few thoughts on each design (primarily the colour scheme). The images are then assessed in a whole-group discussion session.

(Total time needed = 45 minutes)

Good exemplars

1 Germany 1918–1938

The Swastika – in various colours. A session on this symbol could be used to reinforce understanding of Nazi ideology.

A black and white Swastika provoked the following reactions from pupils: 'DEPRESSING', 'EVIL', 'SAD', 'STRONG', 'POWERFUL', 'NOTICEABLE', 'THREATENING', 'DEATH', 'MORBID', 'DARK'

A blue and black Swastika provoked the following reactions from pupils: 'STUPID', 'HARMLESS', 'NEUTRAL', 'HAPPY', 'AQUA', 'FEMININE', 'BRIGHT', 'EVIL', 'STRANGE', 'QUEER', 'BORING'

A red and black Swastika provoked the following reactions from pupils: 'POWERFUL', 'DANGEROUS', 'STRONG', 'INTIMIDATING', 'OPPRESSION', 'FRIGHTENING', 'BOLD', 'VIOLENT', 'IN YOUR FACE', 'BLOODY'

A purple Swastika provoked the following reactions from pupils: 'SOFT', 'PUSHOVER', 'GIRLY', 'SICKLY SWEET!', 'AIRY-FAIRY', 'PALE', 'NON-THREATENING', 'STUPID', 'WEAK', 'ROMANTIC', 'TISSUE PAPER–SOFT AND ABSORBENT!'

A green and yellow Swastika provoked the following reactions from pupils: 'ECO-NAZIS!', 'FREEDOM', 'PITIFUL', 'FRIENDLY', 'KIND', 'WEAK', 'NOT TO BE TAKEN SERIOUSLY'

What issues are raised by this exercise? Why do individuals react in the way they do to different colour schemes? What conclusions can we draw about Nazism – and our perception of it?

How would pupils respond to a 'bold' Communist Hammer and Sickle in pastel green instead of red? Or a 'patriotic' French tricolour in pink, white and yellow? Why is colour so important in history?

Learning outcomes

Following the exercise, class members will be able to: (1) assess the significance of symbolism for movements and organisations; (2) critically review the issue of colour and image in history.

Summary

Merits?

- ☐ Highly provocative.
- ☐ A fun activity which focuses on the often-neglected topic of colour in history.
- ☐ Involves focused practical groupwork.

Possible problem?

- ☐ Participants can be unduly influenced by their prior knowledge of 'real' colour schemes.

Finetuning?

- ☐ To allow more time for discussion and appraisal, the new (strangely coloured) images could be prepared beforehand as posters or as OHP acetates.

ACTIVITY 9

Devise a Board Game

Challenge pupils to create a puzzle

Description

Setting and context

Board games can be extremely useful in helping to visualise key events or developments in history; for example, the rise and fall of empires or the emergence of totalitarian states. Board games can highlight significant issues and bring alive important debates. But beware! This activity comes with a public health warning. Devising and playing games is great fun, but the teacher must exercise strict control over the lesson and ensure that all participants are focused on the intended outcomes of the lesson. May be unsuitable for last period on a Friday!

Learning aims and objectives

To comprehend a key episode in history – and the part played by human and non-human factors.

Resources needed

- [ ] Sugar paper
- [ ] Card
- [ ] Scissors
- [ ] Coloured pens
- [ ] A range of maps, texts and sources

Breakdown of method in action

Time needed	Phase of activity
10 mins	The teacher presents a range of visual sources to the class (texts, maps, images) and asks the pupils to familiarise themselves with the subject topic.
15 mins	Working in small groups, the pupils indicate the kind of data that would help them in devising their game.
10 mins	The teacher explains the devise-a-board-game task.

Rest of the lesson (and maybe a further lesson)	Participants devise and play the games.

(Total time needed = 35 minutes-plus)

Good exemplar

1 *Slavery in America*

After studying slave conditions and rebellions, the pupils are asked to devise a board game that would illustrate the difficulties faced by black American slaves in plotting and successfully carrying out an escape. In this example, the objectives of the session are to enable group members to: (a) use a range of maps, sources and texts in order to visualise certain aspects of slave escapes (routes, difficulties encountered along the way etc); (b) develop groupwork skills; (c) become aware of how futile attempts at escape actually were.

Conventional games can also be adapted to accommodate a certain historical development or event. For example, Snakes and Ladders could be used to chart the rise and fall of the Roman Empire and Monopoly to illustrate the problems of living in cities throughout history – Victorian London or Ancient Rome.

Learning outcomes

At the end of the activity, participants will be able to: (1) understand the complex interaction of people and events in the past; (2) design a learning method that is capable of illuminating key issues and themes in a topic area.

Summary

Merits?

- [ ] Brings a subject alive.
- [ ] Allows class members to 'visualise' an important historical issue – particularly useful in the study of abstract concepts.
- [ ] Encourages empathy and fosters problem-solving skills. Pupils are asked to make choices that will shape world history!
- [ ] In order to produce the board game, individuals have to research the set topic thoroughly.

Possible problem?

- [ ] Thinking that the exercise is 'just a game'. Thus, task-definition must be clear and the value of the activity 'sold' to pupils.

Finetuning?

- [ ] The introduction of time-scales and restraints where the topic area is huge?

ACTIVITY 10

Annotation

Intelligent graffiti

Description

Setting and context

Annotation of a visual source is a good way of encouraging pupils to scrutinise an image in close detail.

Learning aims and objectives

To enable pupils to: (1) appraise a visual source in depth; (2) share ideas orally as part of a wider group.

Resources required

☐ Pens

Breakdown of method in action

Time needed	Phase of activity
10 mins	Following a class discussion and preparatory work, group members annotate the set visual source in groups, circling and underlining key images and phrases and writing a commentary alongside the image.
15 mins	Class discussion follows. What are the key features of the source and what does it tell us?

(Total time needed = 25 minutes)

Good exemplar

1 *Victorian Britain* (see Figure 1r)

To acquire a closer understanding of contemporary Victorian attitudes to Empire, pupils are given a photocopied image of a Jubilee plate celebrating the 50th anniversary of the reign of Queen Victoria. This is annotated in full by class members (Figure 1r).

Figure 1r Victorian Britain.[14]

How would pupils annotate other historical images?

Learning outcomes

On completion of the exercise, pupils will be able to: (1) dissect and interpret a visual source; (2) link analytical comments to specific aspects of an image; (3) critically assess the overall significance of a graphic source.

Summary

Merits?

☐ Universal application – can be used with a whole range of visual sources, including photographs, paintings and cartoons as well as texts.

---

14 C. Shephard and B. Brown, *Britain 1750–1900*, London, John Murray, 1997, p. 237.

☐ Really encourages participants to stop and look in detail at the content of a source.

☐ Allows for a wide range of ideas to be aired about the source.

Figure 1s Inference layer template (see page 56).[15]

---

15 C. Riley, 'Evidential understanding, period knowledge and the development of literacy: a practical approach to layers of inference for Key Stage 3', quoted in D. Laffin, 'A Poodle with Bike: Using ICT to make AS level more rigorous', *Teaching History*, November 2000.

Possible problem?

☐ Fitting it in. This activity is best employed as a catalyst for discussion rather than as a discrete exercise used in isolation.

Finetuning?

☐ Class members may sometimes miss the obvious – so the teacher might like to encourage them to comment only on specific aspects of the image.

☐ The visual could be enlarged and mounted on sugar paper, with pupils using marker pens to annotate the source – a 'messier' approach, but one that might enhance thinking and discussion.

☐ Sources could be mounted on an 'inference layer' template, so as to encourage layers of thinking (Figure 1s).

Further reading

T. Buzan, *The Mindmap Book*, London, BBC Consumer Publishing.

C. Counsell, *Analytical and Discursive Writing at KS3*, London, Historical Association, 1997.

H. Gardner, *The Unschooled Mind: How Children Think and How Schools should Teach*, New York, Basic Books, 1991.

H. Gardner, *Frames of Mind: The Theory of Multiple Intelligences*, London, Montana Publishers, 1993.

H. Gardner, *Multiple Intelligences: The Theory in Practice*, New York, Basic Books, 1993.

J. O'Neill, 'Teaching Pupils to Analyse Cartoons', *Teaching History*, May 1998.

C. Riley, 'Evidential Understanding, Period Knowledge, and the Development of Literacy: A Practical Approach to "Layers of Inference" for KS3', *Teaching History*, November 1999.

D. Sheppard, 'Confronting Otherness: Developing Scrutiny through Drawing', *Teaching History*, August 2000.

B. Walsh, 'Practical Classroom Approaches to the Iconography of Irish History or: How Far Back do we Really Have to Go?', *Teaching History*, May 1999.

Review

Visuals can be of great help in developing conceptual understanding and opening up the past. In addition to analysing and interpreting sources such as photographs, paintings and cartoons, pupils can be challenged to 'visualise' the past via charts, diagrams and images that they produce themselves. This process can stimulate understanding – and can also aid pupils in remembering key dates, people and events. It is in 'seeing the past' that history as a subject really comes alive.

Numerical Data

Adding interest

If you only do what you've always done,

you'll only get what you've always got.

Anonymous

Introduction

This chapter aims to provide teachers with ten distinct ways of provoking small-group discussion when numerical data is the focus of classroom attention. First though, we must clarify what we mean by the phrase 'numerical data'. Here we are talking, primarily, about *tabular* data; in the context of history this could mean tables of electoral figures, economic statistics or even opinion-poll information; in short, any form of historical data presented in tabular mode. The rationale behind this chapter is threefold: to make numerical data more accessible, to help teachers in their efforts to provoke constructive data-orientated discussion, and to enable pupils to comprehend and understand data better. Underlying these three aims is a fourth: to increase the confidence, and enhance the practical classroom options, of teachers who deal with numerical data on a regular basis.

The basic assumption at the heart of this chapter is that many pupils – and staff - do not feel totally comfortable with numerical data. While the former tend to view statistical information with serious suspicion, the latter, it might be suggested, do not generally look forward to teaching topics that include a heavy data element. There just seems to be something innately off-putting about statistical data for many young people and teachers.

The irony of course is that tabular data can be a rich form of historical evidence; it can be useful, provocative and contain vital explanatory details – whatever the topic under consideration. Numerical data can be priceless for historians in search of factual information or argument; hence the importance of stimulating discussion around statistical tables and making them accessible and pupil-friendly. The reality is that in most History syllabi there will come a time when the focus shifts to some form of tabular data. Clearly, in this situation, it is important that teachers are armed with the necessary classroom ideas to provoke discussion and to make the subject matter accessible. The recently launched Numeracy Initiative makes it essential to explore the world of tabular data, and to develop imaginative teaching ideas to cope with it.

Activities

11 Translation (Key Stage 3)

12 Numbers and Letters (Key Stage 3)

13 Worksheet Questions (Key Stage 3)

14 The Debate (AS/A-Level)

15 Slogans and Logos (Key Stage 3)

16 Dream Figures (AS/A-Level)

17 Isolation (GCSE)

18 Roleplay Predictions (GCSE)

19 Implications (GCSE)

20 Newspaper Headlines (Key Stage 3)

The most suitable level for usage is indicated in brackets. However, it should be noted that, with a little adaptation and customisation, many activity ideas contained within this chapter could also be employed at other levels.

Translation

Transform numbers into a diagram or something else

Description

Setting and context

This method is appropriate wherever difficult and complex data is causing problems – where a new and different representation of the data might aid understanding.

Learning aims and objectives

The objectives of the exercise are to: (1) promote discussion by asking pupils to 'translate' data into other more comprehensible forms; (2) appraise the data (in numerical form and in an alternative format); (3) encourage deep understanding among class members.

Resources required

☐ Photocopies of set data
☐ Coloured marker pens
☐ Poster-size paper
☐ Blu-Tack

Breakdown of method in action

Time needed	Phase of activity
5 mins	Teacher outlines aims of session and introduces the main issues under consideration.
5 mins	Pupils are given time to familiarise themselves with the specific piece of data under analysis.
30 mins	Pupils – in mini-groups – are challenged to 'translate' the table of data into three other intelligible forms, whether a diagram, a chart, a map-based graphic, a graphic of some other sort, a newspaper headline, a newspaper editorial, a newspaper report, drama, roleplay … or any other form. They have to imagine that they are 'translating' the data for people who have no understanding of numbers or raw numerical data – and thus, they have to present the numerical information in another way to enlighten them.

10 mins	The teacher chairs a discussion which focuses on the 'translations' produced by the pupils; the main suggestions are presented and the main ideas and themes analysed – and further discussion ensues about the meaning and nature of the data under consideration: what points emerge from the 'translated' material that do not emerge so starkly from the tabular data?

(Total time needed = 50 minutes)

Good exemplars

1 *Britain in the Fourteenth Century*

Some of the amounts that people had to pay as a result of the Poll Tax in 1379.[1]

Duke of Lancaster	133s 4d
Archbishops	133s 4d
Bishops, abbots and priors	80s 0d
Great merchants	20s 0d
Squires	20s 0d
Monks and canons	3s 4d

How could these sets of figures be represented in an alternative form?

A bar chart:

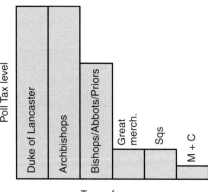

---

1 J. Simkin, *National Curriculum History: Medieval Realms Resource Book*, Brighton, Spartacus Educational, 1991.

A newspaper editorial:

The *Lancashire Times* understands that the Duke of Lancaster will be paying top-level, over-the-odds Poll Tax this year. This is wrong – and we will fight to lessen his burden. Today we ask: Why not tax the Yorkist nobles more?

A drama:

The Duke of Lancaster, an Archbishop, a Bishop, a Merchant, a Squire and a Monk meet together to discuss the Poll Tax levels. Sample conversation:

MERCHANT: Hello, Mr Duke – I think you deserve to pay more. You're a wealthy noble and I have to earn my living.

MONK: My colleagues, the Bishop and the Archbishop, have been targeted – but I've been let off, thankfully. But there again, I'm only a simple monk – I've got no belongings and no property.

ARCHBISHOP: I thought I might be exempt – but no! They really have made me pay!

2 Modern China

Industrial output, by product, 1952–1957[2]

	1952	1957	% increase
Pig iron ('000 tons)	1,900	5,936	212
Steel ('000 tons)	1,348	5,350	297
Coal ('000 tons)	66,490	130,000	96

3 The Second World War

What governments spent on the conflict[3]

Allies	£M	Axis powers	£M
USA	84,500	Germany	68,000
USSR	48,000	Italy	23,500
Britain	28,000	Japan	14,000
Canada	4,000		
France	3,750		
TOTAL	171,250	TOTAL	105,500

2 J.A.G. Roberts, *Modern China: An Illustrated History*, Stroud, Sutton, 2000, p. 227.
3 J. Watson, *Success in Twentieth Century World Affairs*, London, John Murray, 1974, p. 149.

How could the sets of figures in Exemplars 2 and 3 be represented in an alternative form? A graph of some sort? Another type of visual? A newspaper headline, report or editorial? Or could they form the basis of a drama of some kind? The options are endless! The more bold and more daring the approach, the better!

Learning outcomes

At the end of the activity pupils will be able to: (1) assess the meaning of the statistics; (2) evaluate the most significant aspects of the data; (3) show awareness of how statistics can be represented in different forms.

Summary

Merits?

☐ Encourages class members to illustrate the fundamental meaning of statistics via different media.
☐ Makes pupils think, in a focused fashion, about the nature of data.
☐ Enfranchises those pupils who can express themselves creatively and through non-verbal means (although verbal discussion is still central to the activity).
☐ The diversity of translation 'options' e.g. pie charts, newspaper headlines, bar charts, newspaper editorials, some kind of drama.
☐ Brings statistics alive – in concrete fashion.
☐ Appealing hypothetical element e.g. 'Imagine someone can't understand numbers and because of this requires a graphic image or something else to bring out the meaning of stats ...'

Possible problems?

☐ Group members' lack of imagination, creativity and artistic skills.
☐ The 'translation' task subsuming the hoped-for discussion.
☐ Is the whole activity too burdensome on the pupils?

Finetuning?

☐ The mini-groups could be told, explicitly, in what medium or form the teacher wants the statistics to be expressed.
☐ Could an element of roleplay be introduced?

Numbers and Letters

'Doctor' data – and stimulate debate

Description

Setting and context

This activity – in essence, a provocative puzzle-cum-challenge – is a novel teaching and learning device. It would be especially useful where pupils are looking at the particular characteristics of, say, a political party or a national economy. It basically challenges them to identify hidden axes or hidden statistics on the basis of other details on display in a table.

Learning aims and objectives

The objectives of the exercise are to: (1) improve group members' understanding of the subject matter under consideration and to expand their confidence in dealing with numerical data; (2) challenge individuals via a puzzle-style exercise; (3) promote improved learning through competition; (4) increase interest and curiosity about an academic topic.

Resources required

☐ Photocopies of set data
☐ Pens

Breakdown of method in action

Time needed	Phase of activity
5 mins	Teacher introduces session – and its aims.
5 mins	Background issues – general big-group discussion.
15 mins	The class is split up into small groups. The handout is given to the mini-groups and, via a series of 'comprehension' questions attached to the table, each group is challenged to identify the missing names and figures; small-group discussion follows.
10 mins	Teacher reveals answers – then more discussion in big-group (or small-group) context.

(Total time needed = 35 minutes)

Good exemplars

I *Nazism*

The social composition of the Nazi electorate in percentage terms.[4]

Election	1928	1930	July 1932	November 1932	1933
Denomination					
Catholic	30	20	17	17	a
Other or none	70	80	83	83	76
Social group					
b	40	40	39	39	40
Salaried/civil servants	22	21	19	19	18
Independents and farmers	37	39	42	41	42

In small groups, participants address the following:

Question 1: Estimate *a*.

Question 2: What social group is *b*?

(Answers: *a* = 24; *b* = workers)

2 *Stalin*

Annual average production of basic armaments in the USSR, 1930–1940.[5]

Armament type	1930–1	1932–4	1935–7	1938–40
Aircraft	869	2,595	3,758	a
Tanks	740	b	3,139	2,672
c	174,000	256,000	397,000	1,379,000

---

4   C. Fischer, *The Rise of the Nazis*, Manchester, MUP, 1995, p. 171.
5   R.T. Manning, 'The Soviet Economic Crisis of 1936–1940 and the Great Purges' in J. Arch Getty and R.T. Manning, *Stalinist Terror*, Cambridge, CUP, 1994, p. 134.

In small groups participants discuss the following:

Question 1: Estimate *a*.

Question 2: What would you expect *b* to be, approximately?

Question 3: What type of armament is *c*?

(Answers: *a* = 8,805; *b* = 3,371; *c* = rifles)

3 *Britain in the Fourteenth Century*

The adult population of England as recorded in the Poll Tax Accounts of 1377 and 1381.[6]

	1377 – (Edward III) adult population	1381 – (Richard II) adult population
Cornwall	34,274	12,056
Cumberland	11,841	*a*
Derbyshire	23,243	15,637
Devon	*b*	20,656
Dorset	34,241	19,507
Essex	47,962	30,748
Kent	56,307	43,838
c	23,880	8,371
Norfolk	88,797	66,719
Suffolk	58,610	44,635
Surrey	18,039	12,684
Sussex	35,326	26,616
Westmoreland	*d*	3,859

In small groups participants address the following:

Question 1: Predict *a*.

Question 2: Estimate *b*.

Question 3: Which county is *c*?

Question 4: What is *d*, approximately?

(Answers: *a* = 4,748; *b* = 45,635; *c* = Lancashire; *d* = 7,389)

---

6   Simkin, *op. cit.*

Learning outcomes

Following the exercise participants will be able to: (1) assess the main trends in a table of statistics; (2) explain why certain key figures, and axes, are as they are; (3) compare and contrast individual statistics.

Summary

Merits?

- [ ] Competition – can provoke participants into productive classroom activity.
- [ ] Important 'fun' aspect.
- [ ] Pupils learn via the data – and via other pupils' comments.
- [ ] The questions can lead on to discussion about other related issues.

Possible problems?

- [ ] Pre-class preparation – slightly messy and tricky!
- [ ] Competition – can have negative effects on some participants.
- [ ] Ambiguous data can sabotage the whole activity!

Finetuning?

- [ ] An additional roleplay element (post-puzzle) to bring out further aspects of the data?

ACTIVITY 13

Worksheet Questions

Introduce data – and set a comprehension test

Description

Setting and context

This is a simple teaching and learning method, but no less effective for that. It is suitable for any situation in which a class needs to get to the heart of a table of data and its many different facets.

Learning aims and objectives

The objectives of the exercise are to: (1) encourage participants to think about the many different features of a statistical table; (2) focus the minds of class members by asking them for definite written answers to specific questions; (3) promote small-group and big-group debate.

Resources required

☐ Photocopied table of data with worksheet questions attached.
☐ Pens and paper for participants' answers.

Breakdown of method in action

Time needed	Phase of activity
5 mins	Teacher outlines the topic under debate and explains how the session will be structured.
5 mins	Teacher hands out tabular data under consideration and gives pupils time to familiarise themselves with it.
10 mins	Participants are split into mini-groups and asked to consider Questions 1–3.
10 mins	Big-group feedback session – with the mini-groups sharing their answers to Questions 1–3.
10 mins	Individuals go back into their groups and discuss Questions 4–6.
10 mins	Big-group feedback session – with the mini-groups sharing their answers to Questions 4–6 and more general discussion.

(Total time needed = 50 minutes)

Good exemplars

1 *Mussolini*

1913 and 1919 elections.[7]

	Voters 1913	Voters 1919	Seats 1913	Seats 1919
Giolittian Coalition	3,392,000	1,779,000	410	193
War Veterans		320,000		334
Catholics	302,000		29	
Populists		1,167,000		100
Republicans	437,000	581,000		9
Independents	(together)	(together)	17	17
Socialists	883,000	1,835,000	52	156
Total	5,014,000	5,682,000	508	508

Possible worksheet questions

☐ Why did the Giolittian Coalition lose votes between 1913 and 1919?
☐ What is significant about the emergence of the War Veterans group in 1919?
... etc, etc.

2 *Elizabeth I*

The House of origin of Acts 1571–97.[8]

	Acts originating in Commons	Acts originating in Lords	Total Acts
1571	20	20	40
1572	11	6	17
1576	20	17	37
1581	20	9	29
1584	31	17	48
1586/7	6	4	10
1589	15	9	24
1593	15	12	27
1597	32	11	43

7   G. Salvemini, *The Origins of Fascism in Italy*, New York, Harper & Row, 1961, p. 232.
8   M.A.R. Graves, *The Tudor Parliaments*, London, Longman, 1995, p. 139.

Possible worksheet questions:
- [ ] What are the main trends evident in the table?
- [ ] What explains the Commons' growing ascendancy over the Lords?

... etc, etc.

3 Nazism

Statistics on political crimes for 1933.[9]

Nature of offence	No. of those tried (including acquittals)	No. sentenced
High treason	2,000	1,698

Possible worksheet questions:
- [ ] What is high treason?
- [ ] What does this table tell us, in general terms, about Hitler's Germany?

... etc, etc.

Learning outcomes

Following the exercise pupils will be able to: (1) critically analyse the main features of the table; (2) assess and review the main trends in a table of data.

Summary

Merits?

- [ ] Easy to design.
- [ ] Effective in generating discussion.
- [ ] Focuses group thinking.
- [ ] Gives pupils a clear direction.

Possible problems?

- [ ] Narrow questions – the questions need to challenge the pupils, and some actually need to go beyond the table of data.
- [ ] Just 'boring' comprehension?
- [ ] Too many questions?

Finetuning?

- [ ] A set of 'why' questions only?
- [ ] A mixture of 'narrow' data-based questions and 'broader' tangential questions?

---

9 M. Broszat, *The Hitler State*, London, Longman, 1981, p. 332.

The Debate

Use statistics to bring a crucial two-sided argument alive

Description

Setting and content

This classroom activity is appropriate for any situation in which a key academic debate comes under the microscope and in which the teacher wishes to explore the main contours of the debate and a key table of data in an in-depth way.

Learning aims and objectives

The objectives of the exercise are to: (1) promote awareness of the relationship between statistical evidence and key lines of argument in a set debate; (2) stimulate relevant small-group discussion; (3) involve pupils, via roleplay, in a set debate; (4) increase participants' awareness of the significance and potency of numerical evidence.

Resources required

☐ Paper
☐ Pens

Breakdown of method in action

Time needed	Phase of activity
5 mins	Teacher introduces subject matter for debate and outlines the main contours of the session.
5 mins	The pupils – in small groups – are given time to familiarise themselves with the data under scrutiny.
5 mins	The teacher outlines the essay question around which the 'debate' will focus; it becomes clear that there are two main strands to the argument (e.g. on the one hand, reinforcing the set quotation, and on the other, advancing the contrary view).

| 20 mins | Two mini-groups are set up to mirror the two main arguments. One group basically takes the role of 'defence' ('defending' the quotation), while the other plays the part of the 'prosecution' ('attacking' the quotation and trying to undermine it). The teacher meanwhile plays the role of judge and jury. The 'defence' and 'prosecution' are asked to do three things: (1) build up their general case; (2) identify two pieces of statistical evidence from the table which can help them make their case; and (3) advance their argument – and at the same time attempt to deconstruct their opponents' thesis. |
| 15 mins | The teacher chairs a plenary discussion where all the main issues can be debated and where pupils – out of role – can assess the main arguments. |

(Total time needed = 50 minutes)

Good exemplars

1 *The Normans and England 1066–87*

Question to debate: To what extent did royal servants and other officials dominate land-holding in England in 1086?

English tenants-in-chief, 1086.[10]

Edward of Salisbury	312½ hides
Gospatric son of Arnkell	145½ hides
Thorkell of Warwick	132 hides
Colswein of Lincoln	100 carucates
Christina	57¼ hides
Harold son of Earl Ralph	36 hides
Godric dapifer	32 carucates
Colgrim	25¼ carucates
Eadgifu of Chaddesley Corbett	25 hides
Alric the cook	20 hides
Alsige	10 hides
Edgar æthling	8¼ hides
Alfred, Wigot's nephew	8 hides

10 A. Williams, *The English and the Norman Conquest*, Woodbridge, Boydell, 1997.

Mini-group A is asked to argue that royal servants and other officials dominated English land-holding in 1086. Mini-group B is asked to argue against this line of thought. How could the two groups exploit the table for helpful evidence?

2 Nazi Germany

Question to debate: 'There were distinct regional patterns to Nazi Party support in 1933'. Discuss.

The regional strength of the NSDAP, in percentage terms, according to the Reichstag elections of 5 March 1933 (electoral districts of the Reich arranged in order of the National Socialist share of the vote).[11]

East Prussia	56.5
Pomerania	56.3
Frankfurt/Oder	55.2
Hanover East	54.3
Liegnitz	54.0
Schleswig-Holstein	53.2
Breslau	50.2
Chemnitz-Zwickau	50.0
Hesse-Nassau	49.4
Braunschweig	48.7
Mecklenburg	48.0
Hesse-Darmstadt	47.4
Magdeburg	47.3
Thuringia	47.2
Rhineland-Palatinate	47.2
Merseburg	46.4
Franconia	45.7
Baden	45.4
Potsdam I	44.4
Dresden-Bautzen	43.6

---

11 Broszat, *op. cit.*

Oppeln	43.2
Württemberg	42.0
Weser-Ems	41.4
Upper Bavaria-Swabia	40.9
Leipzig	40.0
Lower Bavaria	39.2
Hamburg	38.9
Coblenz-Trier	38.4
Potsdam II	38.2
Düsseldorf East	37.4
Düsseldorf West	35.2
Düsseldorf North	34.9
Westphalia South	33.8
Berlin	31.3
Cologne-Aachen	30.1
In the Reich as a whole	43.9

Mini-group A argues in favour of the quotation. Mini-group B puts the case against it. How could the two groups exploit the table for helpful evidence?

3 Russian Dictatorship 1855–1956

Question to debate: In what sense was there a social and economic basis to the Stalinist purges?

Incidence of purges by birth environment.[12]

Birthplace	Purged	Not purged
Village	85 (56.7%)	65 (43.3%)
Urban area	98 (41.7%)	137 (58.3%)
Total (for whom birthplace is known)	183 (47.5%)	202 (52.5%)

---

12 J. Arch Getty and W. Chase, 'Patterns of Repression among the Soviet Elite', in Arch Getty and Manning, *op. cit.*, p. 232.

Incidence of purges by social origin.[13]

Social origin	Purged	Not purged
Bourgeois	14 (73.7%)	5 (26.3%)
Artisan	15 (71.4%)	6 (28.6%)
Peasant	77 (67.5%)	37 (32.5%)
Noble	18 (47.2%)	20 (52.8%)
Professional	34 (48.6%)	36 (51.4%)
Worker	38 (43.7%)	49 (56.3%)
Employee	12 (42.9%)	16 (57.1%)
Total (for whom father's occupation is known)	208 (55.2%)	169 (44.8%)

Mini-group A says there was a social and economic basis to the purges. Mini-group B disagrees. How could the two groups exploit the table for helpful evidence?

Learning outcomes

At the end of the activity participants will be able to: (1) assess the relationship between numerical evidence and 'line of argument'; (2) critically review the key dynamics in a set table; (3) argue a case with which they may personally disagree.

Summary

Merits?

☐ The roleplay element clarifies the main issues involved.
☐ Number of roles to 'play' can be increased where there are larger groups.
☐ The element of confrontation – it can bring healthy results.
☐ Helps emphasise the relevance of numerical data.
☐ Forces pupils to argue 'lines' they may not necessarily agree with.

---

13 Arch Getty and Chase, *op. cit.*

Possible problems?

☐ Starting the debate off.
☐ Statistical data that are 'too complex'.
☐ An 'unbalanced' or 'one-sided' question: the opening quotation needs to give both sides a decent opportunity to make a case.

Finetuning?

☐ Extra roles to play – judge, jury, etc – if class numbers allow?
☐ Group members to utilise additional statistics in making their case?

ACTIVITY 15

Slogans and Logos

Explore the link between facts, figures and image

Description

Setting and context

This teaching method centres on marketing and propaganda. Mini-groups are challenged to invent realistic slogans and logos; all they have to help them in this chore
is a series of statistics (some more relevant than others). This exercise is best
utilised where a course is examining the main attributes and characteristics of a
particular movement, organisation, or even regime; in essence, any context in
which there is an image to project and where propaganda is a key issue. Thus, this
strategy may be particularly appropriate where any of the following are the focal
point of study: war, political movements, economic corporations or controversial
regimes. Pupils will have to determine how important their set statistics are, and in
what ways they can be used to underpin marketing and advertising.

Learning aims and objectives

The objectives of the exercise are to: (1) improve understanding of a key subject
topic and to enhance the ability to interpret and use statistics; (2) encourage pupils
to represent their ideas in graphic form; (3) promote individuals' awareness of the
importance of image and presentation; (4) assist group members in discerning the
meaning of key statistics; (5) enable pupils to understand how statistics can be
'manipulated' and 'exploited'; (6) provoke relevant small-group and big-group
discussion around the data.

Resources required

- [ ] Five statistics per mini-group (each printed on a small piece of card – with no
accompanying elaboration)
- [ ] Coloured marker pens
- [ ] A3 paper
- [ ] Blu-Tack

Breakdown of method in action

Time needed	Phase of activity
5 mins	Teacher outlines aims of session.
5 mins	Teacher chairs introductory discussion about topic under scrutiny.
20 mins	The mini-groups are given three selected pieces of data about a particular movement or organisation; these pieces of data may be either highly relevant or irrelevant, but, whatever the exact mixture, they have to be duly considered, assessed and then exploited. The pupils are asked to act as advertising executives or marketing agents for the movement/ organisation in question. On the sole basis of the data they are given, they are challenged to produce a range of publicity slogans and logos – propaganda-style material designed to 'sell' the movement/organisation.
10 mins	The class as a whole picks the most effective slogan and logo from the range on offer.
10 mins	Post-exercise discussion: what main points emerge out of the exercise?

(Total time needed = 50 minutes)

Good exemplars

1 *Chartism*

- ☐ In 1842 the Chartists had 48,000 members.
- ☐ Between June 1839 and June 1840 at least 543 Chartists were either imprisoned or detained by the authorities.
- ☐ The Chartists' petition – presented in May 1839 – was 3 miles long, with 11 million signatures.[14]

What slogans and logos would spring from this statistical information?

Possible slogans:

WE'VE SUFFERED – AND WE'LL WIN!

WE WON'T GO THE EXTRA MILE. WE'LL GO THE EXTRA MILES. FOLLOW THE CHARTISTS ON THE ROAD TO VICTORY!

---

14 R. Maples, *Modern British and European History*, London, Letts, 1985, and <http://landow.stg.brown.edu/victorian/history/chartism7.html>.

Possible logo:

$$C^{11}$$

What issues are raised by this logo and these slogans? What kind of discussion would ensue?

2 *The United Nations*

- [ ] In 1945 the UN had 51 member states.
- [ ] In 1992 the UN had 179 member states.
- [ ] The Security Council of the UN has 15 members.

What slogans and logos would spring from this statistical information?

Possible slogans:

UNITED NATIONS – UNITED WE STAND

THE FASTEST GROWING CLUB IN THE WORLD. JOIN THE UN!

Possible logo:

UNBEATABLE

What issues are raised by this logo and these slogans? What kind of discussion would ensue?

3 *Depression and the New Deal in the USA*

- [ ] The Civil Works Administration created four million jobs on public-works projects.
- [ ] Between 1933 and 1935 farm incomes doubled as a product of New Deal policies
- [ ] Overall, the New Deal found work for 10 million unemployed Americans.

What slogans and logos would spring from this statistical information?

Possible slogans:

10 MILLION AMERICANS SAY YES!

DOUBLE YOUR INCOME. BECOME A FARMER!

Possible logo:

What issues are raised by this logo and these slogans? What kind of discussion would ensue?

Learning outcomes

Following the exercise pupils will be able to: (1) explain how numbers can be used and manipulated; (2) critically assess slogans and headlines that are based on statistics; (3) provide insights into the nature of advertising and marketing; (4) be selective in the way they use statistics – using and discarding figures.

Summary

Merits?

- ☐ Novel visual stimuli – which can provoke excellent discussion.
- ☐ Pupils encouraged to see themselves as 'professionals'.
- ☐ Emphasis on image and marketing – very modern and contemporary.
- ☐ Encourages pupils to evaluate and interpret a range of statistics.

Possible problems?

- ☐ Pupils' lack of confidence in their own creative skills.
- ☐ Time constraints – this can be a long-drawn-out exercise.
- ☐ One-dimensional statistics – data need to be rich and varied.
- ☐ The 'means' subsuming the 'end' e.g. the practical task subsuming the discussion.

Finetuning?

- ☐ Groups of at least three people?
- ☐ No drawing – just slogan writing?
- ☐ More post-task discussion time?

Dream Figures

Invent a set of plausible statistics – and take the argument from there

Description

Setting and context

This activity, which incorporates a novel element of statistic-creation, is appropriate for any classroom situation in which the teacher wishes to investigate the relationship between statistical evidence and specific lines of argumentation.

Learning aims and objectives

The objectives of the exercise are to: (1) stimulate relevant and constructive discussion around 'imaginary' statistics; (2) encourage pupils to think about the nature and plausibility of data and about how specific statistics relate to set arguments; (3) promote small-group and big-group discussion; (4) assist participants in exploring different types of statistical evidence.

Resources required

☐ Pens
☐ Index cards
☐ Poster-size paper

Breakdown of method in action

Time needed	Phase of activity
5 mins	Teacher introduces subject matter under discussion and aims of the learning session.
10 mins	Teacher divides the class into three mini-groups and gives them time to think about the main topic for debate.
15 mins	The teacher gives each mini-group a different 'line' to argue and challenges each to devise three 'dream' statistics to help them reinforce their specific argument. The teacher demands two things: that a variety of 'types' of statistic are produced, and also that the 'dream' statistics are plausible.

10 mins	Each group writes its three 'dream statistics' onto a piece of poster-size paper and passes them on to the group to its right. For each group the challenge is to deduce what line of argument the group to the left of them has been given to focus on.

(Total time needed = 40 minutes)

Good exemplars

I *Napoleon I*

'Arguments' given to participants:

(1) 'Napoleon I was the natural heir to the Old Regime.'

'Dream statistics' put forward by Mini-group A:

- ☐ '71% of Napoleon's colleagues in government also held office before 1789.'
- ☐ 'The Emperor's library contained five times as many books on Louis XIV as on Robespierre.'
- ☐ '32% of French people felt that Napoleon's self-identification with revolutionary values was bogus.'

(2) 'Napoleon I was loyal to the values of the French Revolution.'

'Dream statistics' put forward by Mini-group B:

- ☐ 'He made 12 speeches in the period 1799–1801 that made explicit mention of his revolutionary connections.'
- ☐ 'He attended 17 meetings of the Jacobin Club between 1797 and 1799.'
- ☐ 'He used the word "equality" eight times in one set-piece speech in 1799.'

(3) 'Napoleon I was a unique, modern ruler whose regime bore little resemblance to any previous regimes.'

'Dream statistics' put forward by Mini-group C:

- ☐ 'Twice as many books have been written about Napoleon as about Hitler.'
- ☐ 'The Napoleonic Code was exported to 12 European states.'
- ☐ '34% of books on modern European history begin in 1799 rather than 1789.'

2 *The English Civil War 1637–49*

'Arguments' given to pupils (in two, not three, mini-groups):

A 'There were definite geographical patterns of support for the Royalist and Parliamentary causes during the Civil War.'

What 'dream statistics' would Mini-group A put forward?

B 'There were only vague and non-clear-cut patterns of support for the Royalist and Parliamentarian causes during the Civil War.'

What 'dream statistics' would Mini-group B put forward?

3 *The Condition of England 1832–53*

'Arguments' given to participants (in two, not three, mini-groups):

A 'The Reform Act of 1832 altered the British political landscape in the most radical of terms.'

What 'dream statistics' would Mini-group A put forward?

B 'The Reform Act of 1832 had a minimal effect on British politics.'

What 'dream statistics' would Mini-group B put forward?

Note that, although pupils are encouraged to make their statistics as plausible as possible, the aim of the exercise is to provoke discussion rather than produce completely accurate figures.

Learning outcomes

On completion of the activity, the learner will be able to: (1) assess the relationship between statistical evidence and individual arguments; (2) critically review the meaning and plausibility of tabular data.

Summary

Merits?

☐ Intriguing hypothetical, 'make-believe' element.
☐ Encourages participants to think about the connection between 'evidence' and 'argument'.
☐ 'Swapping' of statistics – can be very provocative.
☐ Intended and unintended learning outcomes.
☐ Encourages lateral thinking.
☐ Unusual perspective on the issue of statistical evidence.
☐ Individuals have to use their imagination.
☐ Illustrates how individual statistics can be interpreted in different ways.

Possible problems?

☐ The notion of 'plausible' statistics – this could confuse some pupils.
☐ Individuals not fully understanding what the activity involves; a full introduction is thus required.

Finetuning?

☐ At the end of the session groups could assess the plausibility of other groups' 'dream statistics'.

ACTIVITY 17

Isolation

Pinpoint key statistics – and focus pupils' minds

Description

Setting and context

This classroom exercise is suitable whenever there is a key table of statistical data under consideration. It is particularly useful where specific details in a table of data need to be brought to life and analysed, and where there are interesting figures that need to be highlighted and explained. This exercise challenges pupils to use their judgement and analytical skills, and can provoke excellent small-group debate.

Learning aims and objectives

The objectives of the exercise are to: (1) encourage participants into thinking about individual statistics and, thereby, to encourage them into thinking about the meaning of all figures in a set table; (2) catalyse constructive small-group discussion; (3) equip group members with the confidence to highlight both significant and less-significant features of a table of data.

Resources required

☐ Photocopies of one table of statistical data
☐ Pens (for pupils to mark tables)

Breakdown of method in action

Time needed	Phase of activity
5 mins	Teacher introduces topic under discussion and sets the scene – outlining the aims of the session and the main issues.
5 mins	Pupils – in mini-groups – are given time to familiarise themselves with the table of data under consideration.
5 mins	The pupils are asked to isolate (and circle) any figures in the table which they perceive to be particularly interesting or provocative.
15 mins	Group members are asked to focus intensely on the individual figures they have highlighted. They are challenged to explain them. Why are they as they are?

15 mins	Teacher chairs summing-up session – which evolves into a general discussion about the data and its meaning.

(Total time needed = 45 minutes)

Good exemplars

1 *World War 1*

UK imports of foodstuffs, 1913–18.[15]

Year	Million tons	Index (1913=100)
1913	18.3	100
1914	16.7	92
1915	**17.0**	93
1916	16.3	89
1917	13.8	**75**
1918	11.9	65

'Interesting' figures identified by pupils in bold: how is it possible to explain them?

Pupil efforts:

17.0: 'An out-of-line jump. Maybe they were importing food in mass amounts early on in the conflict – to cope with the hardship to come.'

75: 'A big drop, late on in the war. Maybe the dislocation of the war was having its effect – you could believe it.'

---

15 G. Hardach, *The First World War*, London, Penguin, 1987.

2 Germany 1918–39

Membership of the SA (%).[16]

Class	Occupational group	1925 to Jan 1933	Feb 1933 to Jun 1934
Working classes			
	Agricultural	2.9	**6.0**
	Unskilled	15.4	21.8
	Skilled	35.4	36.7
	Public sector	0.9	1.2
	Apprentices	1.5	0.5
	Servants	0.4	0.1
Subtotal		56.5	**66.3**
Lower middle and middle classes			
	Master artisans	1.3	1.6
	Non-graduate professions	3.3	1.4
	Salaried staff	8.8	7.3
	Civil servants	2.7	4.6
	Soldiers and NCOs	0.0	0.0
	Salesmen and merchants	10.4	5.9
	Farmers	4.3	2.8
	Family helpers	2.1	1.1
Subtotal		32.9	**24.7**

---

16 Fischer, *op. cit.*

Class	Occupational group	1925 to Jan 1933	Feb 1933 to Jun 1934
Upper middle and upper classes			
	Senior salaried staff	0.2	0.2
	Senior civil servants	0.1	0.5
	Military officers	0.0	0.0
	University students	4.1	**1.4**
	Graduate professions	1.2	2.3
	Entrepreneurs	0.2	0.3
Subtotal		5.8	4.7
Unclear			
	Schoolboys and pupils	1.9	3.3
	Retired	0.4	0.1
	Others or no information	2.0	0.7
Subtotal		4.3	4.1
Total		100.0	100.0
Numbers		2,643	2,356

Note that pupils should compare 1925–33 with 1933–4 figures.

'Interesting' figures identified by pupils in bold: how is it possible to explain them?

Pupil efforts:

6.0: 'A big jump – maybe the Nazis, and the SA in particular, had just launched a big recruitment drive in rural areas.'

66.3: 'The SA is recruiting more and more working class people – that's a significant achievement, and one that would help the cause of Nazism in general terms.'

24.7: 'The middle class base of the SA is declining. Is it becoming more and more a radical phenomenon?'

1.4: 'Less pupils are being attracted to the SA. Maybe the young, intellectual element in German society is seeing through the propaganda and the irrationality of Nazi violence – at last.'

3 Russia 1917–41

Historians' grain crop estimates for the USSR by year (in millions of metric tons).[17]

Year	Jasny	Johnson–Kahan	Official Soviet data (Clark: new)	Wheatcroft
1909–13				72.0
1913			80.1	84.0
1920			45.2	50.0
1921			**36.2–42.3**	**42.0**
1922			56.3	54.0
1923			57.4	56.6
1924			51.4	51.4
1925			74.7	72.5
1926			78.3	76.8
1927			72.8	72.3
1928	**73.3**	**73.3**	**73.3**	**73.3**
1929	**71.7**	**71.7**	**71.7**	**71.7**
1930	83.5	83.5	83.5	78.0
1931	66.0	66.0	69.5	68.0
1932	66.4	63.0	69.6	67.0
1933	70.1	67.1	68.4	69.0
1934	72.2	67.3	67.6	72.0
1935	76.6	69.3	75.0	77.0
1936	63.6	60.0	56.1	59.0
1937	96.0	91.9	97.4	**98.0**
1938	75.9	70.7		75.0
1939	82.9			75.0
1940			95.6	86.2

'Interesting' figures identified by pupils in bold: how is it possible to explain them?

Pupil efforts:

36.2–42.3 and 42.0: 'Very low – comparatively. Maybe it was a bad winter, or a political development that affected the general policy of the regime – not sure really.'

---

17 Manning, *op. cit.*

73.3, 73.3, 73.3, 73.3: 'Everybody agrees – wow! There must have been some official statement that was also verified by independent observers. That's no co-incidence!'

71.7, 71.7, 71.7, 71.7: 'Ditto!'

98.0: 'That's the biggest figure in the table. War is approaching, the regime is in overdrive. If I had been asked to predict the year of the highest figure, I would have said some time in the late 1930s – definitely.'

Learning outcomes

On completion of the activity, the learner will be able to: (1) assess the main trends in a table of data; (2) identify and explain the most interesting statistics.

Summary

Merits?

☐ Encourages pupils to differentiate between statistical elements in a table.
☐ Pupils have to scrutinise and analyse information – this can really bring data alive.
☐ Easy to set up – no resources required except photocopied tables, and pens.
☐ Young people are forced to grapple with a key question: What makes a statistic interesting or extraordinary?
☐ Makes pupils assess the specific meaning of specific statistics.

Possible problem?

☐ An unsuitable table – or too many statistics being isolated by pupils.

Finetuning?

☐ Could an element of roleplay be added to this exercise to bring alive the key issues surrounding the 'isolated' figures?
☐ Participants could be invited to isolate only the three most interesting figures.

Roleplay Predictions

Empathise and forecast

Description

Setting and context

This roleplay-style activity – incorporating a large dose of 'prediction' – is designed to improve and uplift any statistically-based session where the aim is to involve pupils in active discussion and to assess the significance of key figures in a table of data.

Learning aims and objectives

The objectives of the exercise are to: (1) provoke pupils into 'predicting' – and thus discussing fully – a range of key statistics; (2) promote small-group and big-group discussion; (3) inject an element of roleplay and prediction into groupwork; (4) encourage class members to think about the meaning and ramifications of statistics.

Resources required

- [ ] A3 paper
- [ ] Coloured marker pens
- [ ] Index cards

Breakdown of method in action

Time needed	Phase of activity
5 mins	Teacher introduces subject matter and outlines aims of session.
5 mins	Mini-groups are created; each is allocated a roleplay part.
10 mins	Each mini-group is allocated three statistics of various types (some helpful, some not so helpful) and asked, on the basis of these, to discuss and predict. Pupils are asked to present their predictions on wall posters (so all members of the group can see them).
10 mins	Teacher reveals results and then chairs big-group discussion about the pertinence and helpfulness – or not – of the data given to groups: Why did the groups make their predictions as they did? Are there any general conclusions to be drawn?

(Total time needed = 30 minutes)

Good exemplars

1 *World War II*

The dead, 1939–45.[18]

Allies	Millions	Axis powers	Millions
USSR	20.0	Germany	4.2
France	0.6	Japan	1.2
USA	0.4	Austria	0.3

Pupils are split into six roleplay groups to reflect the participating countries – but are not shown the data in the table! The 'Soviets' are challenged to predict the USSR figure, the 'Germans' the figure for Germany, and so on. Each group gets a 'mixed bag' of three statistics to help them. For example, the 'Soviets' might get the following:

(1) 'Britain lost 400,000 men in the war.'

(2) 'The USSR lost far more men than any other country.'

(3) 'Germany lost only a fifth of the amount of men lost by the Soviet Union.'

The Soviet group makes its informed estimates, using these three statements as an aid – and the teacher eventually reveals the 'real' figures for the whole class to see. The other groups do likewise, with the help of their own set of clues. Which roleplay group gets closest to the real statistics? Why? What factors helped and hindered the various groups? What general themes and conclusions emerge from the table when it is revealed?

2 *Russia 1917–41*

The nationalities question (1897 census figures %).[19]

Great Russians	44.32
Ukrainians	17.81
Poles	6.31
Belorussians	4.68
Turkic peoples	10.82
Jews	4.03
Others	11.00

---

18 J. Watson, *Success in Twentieth Century World Affairs*, John Murray, London, 1974, p. 149.
19 R. Pipes, 'National Minorities Sought Autonomy and Independence;' in A.E. Adams (ed.), *The Russian Revolution and Bolshevik Victory*, Boston, Heath, 1960, p. 64.

Pupils are split into seven roleplay groups to reflect the racial groups – but are not shown the data in the table! The 'Great Russians' are challenged to predict the Great Russian figure, the 'Jews' the figure for Jews, and so on. Each group gets a 'mixed bag' of three statistics to help them. For example, the 'Jews' might get the following:

(1) 'There are four times as many Ukrainians as Jews in Russia.'

(2) '6.31% of the Russian population are Poles.'

(3) 'The figure for the Jews is very similar to the figure for the Belorussians.'

The 'Jews' make their informed estimates, using these three statements as an aid – and the teacher eventually reveals the 'real' figure for the whole class to see. The other groups do likewise, with the help of their own set of clues. Which roleplay group gets closest to the real-life statistics? Why? What factors helped and hindered the various groups? What general themes and conclusions emerge from the table when it is revealed?

3 USA and USSR as World Superpowers 1945–89

World economic balance (GNP in billion US$).[20]

Year	USA	Japan	West Germany	France	UK	USSR
1952	350	16	32	29	44	113
1960	511	39	71	60	72	201
1966	748	102	123	108	107	288
1972	1,152	317	229	224	128	439

Pupils are split into six roleplay groups: 'Americans', 'Japanese', 'West Germans', 'French', 'British' and 'Soviets' – but are not shown the data in the table! The 'Americans' are challenged to predict the four USA figures, the 'Japanese' the four Japan figures, and so on. Each group gets a 'mixed bag' of three statistics to help them. For example, the 'Americans' might get the following:

(1) 'The UK GNP for 1952 is US$44 billion.'

(2) 'Soviet GNP more than doubled between 1960 and 1972.'

(3) 'The Japanese GNP figure for 1972 is US$317 billion.'

The 'Americans' begin by making their informed estimates, using these three statements as an aid – and the teacher eventually reveals the 'real' figures for the whole class to see. Which roleplay group gets closest to the real-life statistics? Why? What factors helped and hindered the various groups? What general themes and conclusions emerge from the table when it is revealed?

20 C. Brown and P. Mooney, *Cold War to Détente*, London, Heinemann, 1978, p. 164.

Learning outcomes

At the end of the activity participants will be able to: (1) assess the nature and meaning of key statistics; (2) make informed numerical 'predictions' on the basis of historical evidence.

Summary

Merits?

- [ ] Good 'way in' to a topic.
- [ ] The challenge implicit in the 'prediction' element.
- [ ] Pupils have to think hard about the nature of the statistics they are given as 'clues': are they 'red herrings' or are they useful?
- [ ] Significant competitive dimension.
- [ ] Reinforces and enhances learning.

Possible problems?

- [ ] Competition – will it alienate some people and actually take away from the main exercise?
- [ ] Over-familiarity with the subject matter – this activity is most effective when the subject matter is slightly 'foreign'.

Finetuning?

- [ ] Give individual statistics to group members – rather than giving several to the group as a whole.

ACTIVITY 19

Implications

Think about the consequences of key statistics

Description

Setting and context

This strategy is suitable for any situation in which the teacher wishes to highlight certain specific statistics in a table of data and, furthermore, actually wants to induce discussion about their particular meaning. This exercise also introduces an element of 'make believe' in an effort to provoke group members even further.

Learning aims and objectives

The objectives of the exercise are to: (1) catalyse discussion and stretch pupils' minds around the significance and implications of certain statistics; (2) provoke small-group and big-group discussion; (3) assist pupils in their thinking about the meaning of individual statistics – not the table as a whole; (4) take young people beyond 'reality' – and to test their analytical skills via the consideration of hypothetical data.

Resources required

☐ Photocopies of data
☐ A4 paper and pens

Breakdown of method in action

Time needed	Phase of activity
5 mins	The teacher introduces subject matter and nature of teaching method to be employed.
5 mins	The pupils in small groups are given time to familiarise themselves with the numerical data under consideration.
10 mins	The teacher pinpoints two different statistics in the table and challenges individuals to assess the implications of each and the ramifications of the three together.
10 mins	Big-group discussion: participants share their thoughts.

10 mins	(Optional) The teacher sets another challenge: the pupils have to alter two figures in the table; then they pass the table of data on to another of the participant groups; each group predicts the 'implications' of the 'doctored' figures it receives.

(Total time needed = 30/40 minutes)

Good exemplars

1 *World War I*[21]

	No. of people mobilised per 1,000 of population	No. of people killed per 1,000 of population
France	168	**34**
UK	125	16
Germany	**154**	30

Question for pupils: What are the implications of the figures in bold?

Sample of pupils' ideas:

France 34: 'Indicates that France suffered the most and shows they'd want enormous revenge after the war. It would be a massive landmark in their national history – with a huge legacy.'

Germany 154: 'Shows that Germany invested a significant amount of manpower in the conflict. After the war, and on the back of defeat, there would be a vast array of disillusioned ex-servicemen – a pool of people that would see hope in Nazism?'

2 USA and USSR as World Superpowers 1945–89

The nuclear balance 1964–74.[22]

	Type of missiles	1964	1966	1968	1970	1972	1974
USA	ICBM	**834**	904	1054	1054	1054	1054
	SLBM	416	592	656	656	656	656
	LR bombers	630	630	545	550	455	437

21 J-J. Becker, *The Great War and the French People*, Oxford, Berg, 1993, p. 7.
22 Brown and Mooney, *op. cit.* p. 161.

	Type of missiles	1964	1966	1968	1970	1972	1974
USSR	ICBM	200	300	800	1300	1527	**1575**
	SLBM	120	125	130	280	560	720
	IC bombers	190	200	150	150	140	140

Question for pupils: What are the implications of the figures in bold?

Sample of pupils' ideas:

USA ICBM (1964) 834: 'Shows that when it comes to long-range missiles, 4,000 miles plus, the USA had a big early advantage and inevitably provoked the USSR into a response.'

USSR ICBM (1974) 1575: 'The Soviets had caught up. This sudden achievement would have sent shockwaves through Western capitals. The figure says the USSR really meant business – and would maybe hasten the day when international treaties limiting the build-up were signed.'

3 Germany 1918–39[23]

Those employed	In the Reich (1925 census, %)	In the NSDAP prior to 14 Sep 1930 (%)	Among new NSDAP members (between 14 Sep 1930 and 30 Jan 1933)
Workers	45.1	**28.1**	33.5
Agriculture and forestry (farmers)	6.7	14.1	13.4
Industry and handicraft (artisans and employed in manufactur-ing)	5.5	9.1	8.4
Trade and commerce (tradesmen)	3.7	8.2	7.5
Free professions	1.5	3.0	3.0

23 Broszat, op. cit.

Those employed	In the Reich (1925 census, %)	In the NSDAP prior to 14 Sep 1930 (%)	Among new NSDAP members (between 14 Sep 1930 and 30 Jan 1933)
Public servants Teachers	1.0	1.7	1.7
Others	3.3	6.6	5.5
White collar workers	15.9	**25.6**	22.1
Domestic employees (mostly female)	17.3	3.6	4.9

Questions for pupils: What are the implications of the figures in bold?

Sample of pupils' ideas:

Workers 28.1: 'Shows that, in proportional terms, workers didn't flock to the NSDAP. This would affect the rhetoric of the party in that it might place a bigger emphasis on workers' issues in an attempt to woo them. Shows also the cross-sectional nature of the movement and, arguably, the hollowness of the "socialist" dimension to Nazi policy.'

White collar workers 25.6: 'That's a massive recruitment figure – it would have given the Nazis massive confidence and also influenced their policy ideas.'

Summary

Merits?

☐ Individuals learn from others.
☐ A provocative 'make-believe' element.
☐ Takes pupils beyond the statistics in question.
☐ Transfers 'ownership' of session to the pupils.

Possible problems?

☐ Class members not thinking laterally enough about the possible implications of a certain numerical figure.
☐ Managing the statistics 'swap' effectively.

Finetuning?

☐ Ask the pupils themselves to pick the first group of statistics to be analysed?

ACTIVITY 20

Newspaper Headlines

Attach headlines to data – and watch discussion begin

Description

Setting and context

This learning method is ideal for any context in which the fundamental aim is to seek out the message contained in a set of figures and to consider the way in which the media can put a specific 'gloss' or 'slant' on data.

Learning aims and objectives

The objectives of the exercise are to: (1) analyse the meaning of data via a consideration of how different newspapers might report the release of a certain set of statistics; (2) provoke stimulating classroom discussion; (3) inquire into the essence of media bias; (4) encourage participants to express their ideas in simple (but vivid) newspaper headline form.

Resources required

- ☐ A3 poster-size paper
- ☐ Felt-tip marker pens
- ☐ Blu-Tack

Breakdown of method in action

Time needed	Phase of activity
5 mins	Teacher outlines aims of session.
5 mins	Teacher hands out a table of data – and there is an introductory big-group discussion about this material.
20 mins	Mini-groups are challenged to analyse the data and produce newspaper headlines to accompany the data (each group is given a newspaper title – it could be a real one, it could be make-believe! – and asked to devise headlines from the perspective of that publication).
15 mins	The newspaper headlines – written up in felt-tip on poster-size paper – are displayed on the wall and analysed; there is discussion about the

appropriateness of the headline, the nature of the statistic and the political colour of the newspaper involved.

(Total time needed = 45 minutes)

Good exemplars

I *World War I*[24]

	No. of men killed in action	No. of overall casualties (killed in action, missing, fatally wounded, killed in accidents, by disease, etc)
France	898,000	1,327,000
UK	485,000	715,000
Germany	1,473,000	2,037,000

The date is 1 January 1919 – the overall figures are released to the press. The class is divided into four mini-groups:

☐   The Paris *Express*
☐   The London *Times*
☐   The Berlin *Post*
☐   The *New York Times*

Each of the four groups is asked to analyse the data from 'their' publication's point of view – and then produce appropriate front-page headlines to reflect the 'news' (and the paper's perspective on it). What headlines would each group come up with?

Sample headlines:

The Paris *Express*: FRENCH BLOOD WINS WAR FOR ALLIES

The Berlin *Post*: TWO MILLION CASUALTIES – AND DEFEAT!

... etc, etc.

What kind of discussion would these headlines provoke?

---

24 Becker, op. cit..

2 *Gladstone*

General Election, November 1868

Conservatives 274

Liberals 384

It's the morning after the election. Late editions of the morning newspapers are carrying the story of the Liberals' triumph. The class is divided into three mini-groups:

☐ The Tory *Telegraph*
☐ The Liberal *Lion*
☐ The *Independent*

Each of the three groups is asked to analyse the data from 'their' publication's point of view – and then produce appropriate front-page headlines to reflect the 'news' (and the paper's perspective on it). What headlines would each group come up with?

Sample headlines:

The Tory *Telegraph*: LIBERAL LANDSLIDE – BRITAIN BEWARE!

The Liberal *Lion*: GOTCHA! GOLDEN GLADSTONE ERA BEGINS!

The *Independent*: COUNTRY SWINGS LIBERAL AS TORIES LICK WOUNDS

What kind of discussion would these headlines provoke?

3 *The Cold War*

The armed forces of the great powers in the mid-1970s.[25]

Country	Total armed forces	Total armed forces – as percentage of men of military age
Britain	345,000	3.4
France	502,500	4.9
USSR	3,525,000	6.8
China	3,000,000	1.7
USA	2,174,000	5.5

The class is divided into four mini-groups.

☐ The London *Times*

---

25 Brown and Mooney, *op. cit.*, p. 175.

☐ The Paris *Express*
☐ *Pravda*
☐ The *Chinese People's Daily*
☐ The *New York Times*

Each of the five groups is asked to analyse the data from 'their' publication's point of view – and then produce appropriate front-page headlines to reflect the 'news' (and the paper's perspective on it). What headlines would each group come up with?

Sample headlines:
The London *Times*: AMERICA WILL DEFEND US!
The *China People's Daily*: US AND USSR – WE'RE WATCHING YOU!
… etc, etc.
What kind of discussion would these headlines provoke?

Learning outcomes

Following the activity pupils will be able to: (1) assess the main trends in a table of statistics; (2) critically evaluate numerical data from a variety of perspectives.

Summary

Merits?

☐ Encourages pupils to think clinically and to pick out the main message from the statistics.
☐ Interesting graphic element – a set of newspaper headlines produced by the class, and on display, can inspire a whole new round of discussion.
☐ Reinforces important themes.
☐ Intriguing mix of small-group discussion, roleplay and visual representation.
☐ Modern and contemporary – many young people will enjoy, and adapt to the challenge of, headline-writing.

Possible problems?

☐ The headline-writing task – could it subsume the discussion?
☐ Individuals may find it hard to elicit a simple headline from rows of complicated data – but they should be encouraged!
☐ Pupils' initial lack of awareness of the political line of specific newspapers.

Finetuning?

☐ The pupils could be asked to supply not just headlines, but also editorials – and even cartoons – to illuminate their statistics.

Further reading

P. Harling, *100s of Ideas for Primary Maths*, London, Hodder & Stoughton, 1987
R. Hubbard, *53 Interesting Ways to Teach Mathematics*, Bristol, TES, 1990.
C. Marsh, *Exploring Data*, Cambridge, Polity, 1995.
'Statistics and History Teaching', *Teaching History*, June 1984.

Review

In this chapter, ten distinct teaching methods have been introduced. If the key objectives are to enhance interpretation and evaluation skills, the activities outlined and explained can unlock many doors. Together, they form a kind of 'menu', to be utilised selectively. Obviously some of the activities could benefit from finetuning, the odd minor improvement, or an alternative approach. But, the point made throughout is that the methods are workable. Their main merit is that they can make numerical data *more* accessible and *less* intimidating; they also have the ability to provoke meaningful and constructive classroom discussion. Of course, the majority of the activities require significant pre-planning – but they also have the potential to take discussion and learning onto a different plane.

Concepts

Making them real

The turtle only makes progress when its neck is
stuck out.

(Rollo May)

Introduction

This chapter examines a range of approaches that can be used to enliven teaching
sessions devoted to the study of what pupils might see as 'abstract concepts'. As
historians, of course, we appreciate the importance of theories, models and ideas
to an understanding of our world. However, many young people see the 'facts' set
out in empirical or descriptive terms as the core material of History as a discipline.
While it is difficult to disagree completely with this assessment, any account of
historical phenomena has got to take account of concepts and ideas. Moreover, it
could be argued that many historical conflicts have been fought over values that,
whatever we think of them, cannot simply be ignored. Finally, and perhaps more
importantly, attention to debates over theories and concepts helps us to get some
impression of the 'Big Picture' and to make sense of those actions of states and
individuals that are of interest to pupils in the first place.

Unlike statistics or physics, the key to understanding ideas is not intelligence, but
imagination. The connection between two sets of events, or an understanding of,
say, the Crusades, can suddenly appear to us out of nowhere if we can examine a
situation from another perspective. This mental process requires activity on the
part of the pupil, and generating a 'buzz' in the classroom is the essential trigger for
this. It reduces the pupil's sense of isolation. He or she is no longer trying to figure
it all out alone. Classroom activity is novel and often more interesting than the
digestion of dry textual matter. However, when it produces a spark of imagination
that solves a theoretical riddle, the entire conceptual framework outlined in an
earlier class can simply fit into place. This chapter outlines several exercises that
are capable of having this effect. Our aim has been to find approaches to the
teaching of concepts and abstract ideas which, through classroom activity and
discussion, will light, not so much a spark of genius, but that spark of imagination
in our pupils. This is an ongoing challenge. The exercises below are just the beginning.

Activities

21 Connections (Key Stage 3)

22 Trial by Jury (Key Stage 3)

23 Optical Illusions (Key Stage 3)

24 Root Ideas (Key Stage 3)

25 National Territory (GCSE)

26 Collage (Key Stage 3)

27 Exploring Dilemmas (AS/A-Level)

28 Spatial Mapping (AS/A-Level)

29 Theory and Practice (GCSE)

30 Genealogies (GCSE)

The most suitable level for usage is indicated in brackets. However, it should be noted that, with a little adaptation and customisation, many activity ideas contained within this chapter could also be employed at other levels.

ACTIVITY 21

Connections

Manipulate concepts

Descriptions

Setting and context

This activity is apt for any situation in which pupils are confronted by a range of different and distinct concepts. It can familiarise young people with a range of concepts that might otherwise remain quite remote.

Learning aims and objectives

The objectives of the exercise are to: (1) assist in making concepts more immediate and accessible; (2) promote dexterity in the way that pupils think about, and show relationship between, different ideas.

Resources required

☐ Small cards
☐ Pens

Breakdown of method in action

Time needed	Phase of activity
5 mins	The teacher introduces cards with concepts written on them. There might, for example, be four cards – each bearing a different concept.
10 mins	The class is split up into four mini-groups; each group receives one card to focus on. They are asked to define their idea. One member of each group takes notes.
15 mins	Mini-groups pair up so that there are now two groups in the classroom (each of these groups will now have two cards). Pupils reintroduce their ideas in the larger group. The challenge is to make connections and distinctions between the two concepts. Again, one person in each group will be making notes.
15 mins	The two groups become one – with four cards to play with. The four cards are laid out on a table or on the floor or even fixed to the wall. With the teacher chairing the discussion, pupils are encouraged to make links and connections between the concepts. Can they be put in some kind of order?

Is there a natural hierarchy of ideas? What are the major links and relationships? The teacher asks class members to summarise the main things that have come out of the activity.

(Total time required = 45 minutes)

Good exemplars

1 *Socialism*

The four cards feature the following terms:

FABIANISM

NATIONALISM

NEW UNIONISM

EQUALITY

How would pupils define and manipulate these concepts? How do they relate to the core concept of 'socialism'.

2 *Industrialisation and changes in agriculture*

If the class were exploring industrialisation and modernisation, terms such as these might feature on the cards:

FEUDALISM

ARISTOCRACY

MIDDLE CLASS

URBANISATION

3 *Revolution*

This is suitable for course elements on the American Revolution, the Glorious Revolution or the Revolutions of 1848. The concept list might include:

POLITICAL CHANGE

ELITE

PEOPLE

FREEDOM

Learning outcomes

At the end of the session pupils will be able to: (1) make sense of a variety of abstract concepts; (2) manipulate ideas – comparing them, contrasting them, and relating them to other ideas.

Summary

Merits?

☐ The exercise contains an important visual element – pupils can 'see' relationships and connections.

☐ Concepts are externalised – so making them more accessible.

☐ The activity begins in small groups and ends in a 'big group' plenary – a nice mixture.

☐ Pupils share knowledge and ideas with others; thus, there is a nice communal feel to the whole activity.

Possible problem?

☐ Recording observations: a lot of good small-group point-making could be lost if the note-taker in each group is not conscientious.

Finetuning?

☐ With a particularly able class, the teacher might like to throw in the odd 'rogue' concept, just to keep participants on their toes.

ACTIVITY 22

Ideas on Trial

Explore the consequences of competing arguments

Description

Setting and context

Key concepts or ideas are put 'on trial' in a classroom tribunal. Pupils must prepare a prosecution and a defence, as well as supporting evidence, and judge the contribution of the concept in question to historical events or our understanding of the social world. The adversarial approach to political argument is also explored. Many core concepts used in the study of History lend themselves to vigorous classroom debates. These permit each side to put its case, but pupils tend to be less thorough when it comes to analysis and scrutiny of the opposing arguments. This exercise invites pupils to put concepts, rather than individuals, on trial. A series of charges are drawn up and those who defend the concept must respond to each one. Moreover, the protagonists can call witnesses, living or dead, to make their case. Each side can cross-examine these witnesses and must sum up their positions at the end. It is also possible to extend the exercise by having a 'jury' to consider the evidence and vote on a verdict. It is particularly instructive to allow some discussion on the merits of a two-way confrontation as a means of addressing the issue in question. For instance, on reflection, pupils might conclude that there were more than two sides to the issue and that a black-and-white verdict would be inappropriate. This, of course, is as much a part of the learning process as the handling of the content of the case.

Learning aims and objectives

The objectives of the exercise are to: (1) stimulate pupils into thinking about the role of ideas in History, as opposed to narrative accounts of people and events, and to promote critical engagement with opposing ideas, in place of a blindly polemical approach; (2) utilise the relatively formal setting of a trial or tribunal to structure discussion of conceptual issues; (3) encourage class members to listen to, and engage with, opposing views which they might otherwise ignore; (4) provide individuals with a better understanding of the ideas or concepts on trial and their relationship to historical events.

Resources required

☐ Spacious classroom
☐ Pens

☐ Paper
☐ Visual images, charts or any other items brought by pupils.

Breakdown of method in action

Time needed	Phase of activity
5 mins	Teacher introduces subject matter and outlines aim of session.
10 mins	Prosecution and Defence: opening arguments.
10 mins	Prosecution witnesses and cross-examination.
10 mins	Defence witnesses and cross-examination.
5 mins	Closing arguments from both sides.
5 mins	Consideration of evidence; then verdict.
5 mins	Debriefing: discussion of lessons learned.

(Total time needed = 50 minutes)

Good exemplars

1 *Monarchy*

This debate could be used to consolidate material from several components of the Key Stage 3 syllabus, e.g. Charles I, Cromwell, the Glorious Revolution, the American Revolution or the Revolutions of 1848. It could be undertaken at the end of the course, perhaps as a revision aid. Defenders of monarchy could point to the excesses of Cromwell and to the case for the Glorious Revolution. Critics might look at Charles I or other evidence.

2 *Empire*

This could be a case study of the British Empire and its impact on non-European societies. Defenders might point to elements of modernisation that came with European contact, the passing on of democratic values or the concept of *Pax Britannica*. Critics might refer to slavery, exploitation, racial prejudice and the relative arrogance of the European powers. In an alternative approach, the tribunal might be asked to investigate who bore the guilt for the ill-effects of imperialism – individual British leaders? the military? capitalists? missionaries? These explorations would help with such components of the syllabus as the Development of Empire and the Slave Trade. At Key Stage 3, one would not expect detailed arguments, but, with some intervention from the teacher, it would be possible to raise learners' awareness of more than one way of seeing Britain's imperial role.

3 War

This could be a survey and revision exercise at the end of the Key Stage 3 cycle, bringing together material from such elements of the syllabus as World War I, World War II, Nazism, the UN, Gandhi and Martin Luther King. The Prosecution could cite the philosophies of King and Gandhi, point to the horrors of war and could refer to World War I, the emergence of nuclear weapons or Hitler's militarism. They would suggest that war causes more problems than it resolves. The Defence might argue that only war could have stopped Hitler or point to the prevalence of war in history and the need for vigilance and a will to defend oneself.

Learning outcomes

On completion of the exercise, individuals will be able to: (1) balance the competitive and confrontational aspects of debate with the need to respect one another and engage in orderly discussion; (2) critically analyse their opponents' arguments rather than simply relying on the repetition of their own; (3) understand the debate about the concepts under study.

Summary

Merits?

- [ ] Provides a structure for debate and discussion.
- [ ] Encourages pupils to engage with the arguments of others, rather than simply focusing on their own.
- [ ] Fosters teamwork and, therefore, increased participation.
- [ ] Requires quick thinking and careful planning.
- [ ] Helps to focus attention on ideas rather than merely on personalities and events.

Possible problems?

- [ ] Will not work without considerable pre-class preparation.
- [ ] Risks over-simplification of issues.
- [ ] If the class is not well prepared, the adversarial format could make it too confrontational. There are more than two sides to some debates.
- [ ] Although it could be run in a one-hour class, a thorough treatment of complex issues would require more time.

Finetuning?

- [ ] Further participation and greater variety could be introduced by setting aside time and exercises for the judge and jury, as well as for those conducting the case.

ACTIVITY 23

Optical Illusions

Seeing things differently

Description

Setting and context

This exercise uses optical illusions and aspects of psychology to help pupils explore not only what they learn, but also how they come to an understanding of concepts in history. The activity is based around the sorts of images used in gestalt psychology and their application to the study of the subjectivity of some (or all) social knowledge. The use of such images is not new. It is generally employed to make pupils aware of the potential for seeing things through another lens. Native American and White settlers, for instance, had radically different interpretations of the expansion of the United States across North America in the 19th Century because they come from different starting points, e.g. different opening assumptions about whether land could be fenced in and owned by governments or private individuals. Mere awareness of 'different ways of seeing' can be a useful trigger for a better understanding of History at any level, even Key Stage 3.

Learning aims and objectives

The objectives of the exercise are to: (1) encourage individuals to compare and contrast different ways of understanding history, especially forms of knowledge which are open to competing interpretations and 'factual' knowledge around which there is a general consensus; (2) encourage an exploration of the similarities between the forms of knowledge used in the exercise and those encountered by young people in their study of history; (3) alert pupils to 'different ways of seeing things' in history; (4) provide pupils with an introduction to relatively complex topics, using exercises that are both 'fun to do' and genuinely instructive.

Resources required

☐ Photocopies of illustrations such as Figure 3a.
☐ Paper/pens

Breakdown of method in action

Time needed	Phase of activity
5 mins	Teacher introduces subject matter and outlines aim of session.

5 mins	Pupils are arranged into small groups; groups are given copies of Figure 3a (the duck–rabbit image). The class as a whole discusses the implications of their exercise for how we study history. They can discuss how history might be written by different groups.
15 mins	Small-group discussion on topic in question. Teacher circulates.
10 mins	Groups feed back their ideas.

(Total time needed = 35 mins)

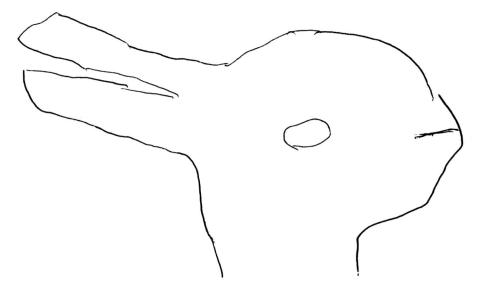

Figure 3a Duck–Rabbit image.

Good exemplars

1 *Salahdin and the Crusades*

Group members are given an image of a duck–rabbit (Figure 3a) and divided into groups. Each group describes its interpretation of the image. Is it a duck? A rabbit? Both? The class is then divided into two groups. The first tells the story of the Crusades from a Western Christian perspective, as the reconquest of the Holy Land from Muslim invaders. The second tells the story from the perspective of the Muslims, ie a story of Westerners invading the Middle East and establishing a foothold there. At the end of the class, class members are asked to identify facts on which both sides would agree (e.g. the Holy Land was invaded), but also list conflicts of interpretation (e.g. about the character of the invaders or their purpose). To focus on the conceptual aspects of history, they should be asked to provide one or two words that would summarise the picture of events held by Muslims and Christians — e.g. 'crusade', 'invasion', 'attack', 'rescue'. Some of these could be suggested by the teacher in order to maintain momentum in the class.

2 *The American Revolution*

The exercise with the duck–rabbit images is conducted as before. The American Revolution can then be described by two groups of pupils, one presenting it as seen from the perspective of London and another from that of the American colonists. In conceptual terms, we end up with a contest between loyalty and legitimate rebellion, themes in the interpretations of all revolutions.

3 *Oliver Cromwell*

Was Cromwell a tyrant or a liberator? Even where the facts are agreed, his intentions and the consequences of his policies for various groups in society left his project open to competing interpretations. This is an excellent case for playing with our sense of perspective. At this level, pupils need not know all the nuances of the debate, but, as long as they can bring bits of evidence to bear, the exercise will expose them to the existence of such a debate in the first place.

Learning outcomes

Following the exercise pupils will be able to: (1) have some sense of the extent to which we view the world through filters dictated by 'ways of seeing' history; (2) understand the distinction between generally agreed facts and areas of disputed interpretation; (3) show awareness of the need to study 'how we know' what we think we understand intrinsically.

Summary

Merits?

☐ The early part of exercise contains a 'mystery' element: the relevance of the duck–rabbit image to political history is not immediately apparent. Yet, because playing with images is entertaining, pupils are keen to 'figure it all out'.

☐ The image stimulates debate and so breaks the ice for more difficult discussion of paradigms. Nobody feels intimidated when talking about rabbits?

Possible problems?

☐ When done at Key Stage 3 level, there will be a need for teacher intervention to explain how a single image could be seen in more than one way or to prompt pupils with words to describe competing interpretations or ideas.

☐ Works best when group members are already familiar with some discussion of competing perspectives on events; advance knowledge of cases being used is important.

Finetuning?

☐ The teacher may need to give participants sufficient background knowledge and provide hints or assistance to those who find concepts difficult to understand.

ACTIVITY 24

Root Ideas

Defining and debating core concepts

Description

Setting and context

This classroom strategy requires pupils to define key concepts which they will come across in their courses, but also to dig deeper and list other related concepts that are important to an understanding of the ones under scrutiny. The ensuing debate over the relative meaning of terms which most take for granted will stimulate further discussion. Pupils are often content to learn key definitions by rote without reflecting on their real meaning. This exercise helps them to get behind the central ideas by exploring related concepts, which are often more important than the one under initial study, by linking them to historical context and people. Pupils will need a variety of supporting materials to help them develop their understanding of concepts.

Learning aims and objectives

The objectives of the exercise are to: (1) encourage participants to reflect on the definitions of core concepts used in history; (2) generate class discussion and debate about the relationship between core ideas, movements or concepts in political history; (3) help class members go beyond core concepts by seeking out and exploring related and underlying ideas.

Resources required

- [ ] Multiple worksheets
- [ ] Pens
- [ ] A3/A4 paper
- [ ] English dictionaries, historical dictionaries or an encyclopedia

Breakdown of method in action

Time needed	Phase of activity
5 mins	Teacher introduces lesson plan.
5 mins	Individuals are broken up into groups.

15 mins	Each pupil is asked to list, and define, a fixed number of concepts that would be essential to a basic understanding of some major theme in a given discipline, such as feudalism, democracy or nationalism.
10 mins	Groups exchange their work and query the rationale for each other's choices and definitions.
10 mins	Wider class discussion about importance of concepts in history and of sources of disagreement over definitions.

(Total time needed = 45 minutes)

Good exemplars

1 *Feudalism and related concepts*

This would be particularly useful in the study of the Peasants' Revolt, Europe in the Time of Charlemagne, Industrialisation and Changes in Agriculture (Key Stage 3). The class is divided into groups of two or three, and they set to work on 'deconstructing' feudalism as a concept. After 15 minutes, the groups exchange sheets and are asked to circle words within the text of the entries offered by others that they think also require a definition. The teacher may have to intervene to prompt for definitions or to assist with difficult concepts.

Group A's work on feudalism:

FEUDALISM (medieval type of economic arrangement involving
master and slave)

↓

SUPERIOR (term used to describe the senior partner in a feudal
relationship)

↓

VASSAL (word used to describe the junior, exploited partner in a
feudal relationship)

↓

HOMAGE (type of exaggerated respect that the vassal must have
for a superior)

↓

PEASANT (worker on the land – similar to vassal)

When Group B receives this short glossary of feudalism, it circles the following words ...

'FEUDAL RELATIONSHIP', 'SLAVERY', 'EXAGGERATED RESPECT'

... and asks Group A to explain these terms.

Group B might also ask Group A a couple of questions. For example:

1   Is 'landlord' another name for 'superior'?

2   What is the difference between a vassal and a peasant?

It's up to Group A, with help from the teacher, to explain.

2 *Stalinism*

This concept requires some knowledge of Stalin's personality and governing style. It also requires an understanding of the concept of 'Communism', which, in turn, requires a definition of 'socialism'. Each definition triggers an exploration of further concepts. This could be useful for the syllabus component on Stalin (World Study after 1900).

3 *Civilisation*

A revision concept linking elements of the Key Stage 3 syllabus, especially those devoted to non-European cultures (Qing Dynasty/Imperial China/Moghul India/Salahdin and the Crusades). The point of this exercise would not be to provide a comprehensive definition of 'Civilisation', but simply to alert pupils to the idea that 'civilisation' cannot simply be equated with Western civilisation, that other cultures have long-established and deep-rooted world-views and traditions as well. By following up the 'buzz words', the teacher can help the class to gain a general understanding of the concept in its broadest sense.

Learning outcomes

At the end of the activity, participants will be able to: (1) explore more fully a range of core concepts they once took for granted; (2) appreciate the value of ideas as guides to understanding history.

Summary

Merits?

- [ ] Encourages pupils to think and to confer in groups.
- [ ] Fosters debate on deeper concepts.
- [ ] Promotes questioning of initial assumptions.

Possible problems?

☐ The activity is dependent on reading and absorption of basic historical facts. The concepts are used to interpret or understand these facts.

Finetuning?

☐ The possible addition of prompt sheets or guides to help weaker pupils and to provide momentum to the class? These could contain provocative information, as well as positive prompting, simply to stir up more discussion.

ACTIVITY 25

National Territory

Exploring a concept with maps

Description

Setting and context

In this exercise, pupils are given blank or partially-labelled maps of a significant region of the world in a particular historical setting. The maps show 21st-Century boundaries. Group members are encouraged to delineate historically significant regions by drawing new boundaries incorporating groups of countries with a common history or which were part of a single empire. The groups must justify their boundaries with reference to key events, ideas or periods. The maps may include prompts, such as present-day indicators of religious or cultural legacies derived from these historical phenomena.

Learning aims and objectives

The objectives of the exercise are to: (1) encourage an awareness of the territorial and cultural expanse of historical political entities and their impact on 21st-Century politics; (2) raise awareness of the impact of historical developments on our sense of region and place; (3) explore the issue of continuity and change in the territorial configuration of key world regions; (4) promote discussion about these issues through individual group activity.

Resources required

☐ Pre-prepared maps showing contemporary state boundaries
☐ Pens
☐ Coloured marker pens
☐ Notepaper
☐ History textbooks and/or several good historical atlases

Breakdown of method in action

Time needed	Phase of activity
5 mins	Brief introduction, explaining what each pupil must do. In real teaching situations, this would normally be undertaken at the end of the previous teaching session.

15 mins	Class is organised into groups (optional); maps distributed. Groups work on maps.
5 mins	Pupils exchange maps: each group justifies its boundary regions.
10 mins	Discussion of boundaries.
10 mins	Discussion of implications of the exercise.

(Total time needed = 45 minutes)

Good exemplars

1 *Multi-national empires*

The concept of multi-national empires is essential to any basic understanding of European history before 1918. Maps can be useful tools in presenting and explaining the concept. In the map in Figure 3b, pupils are asked to identify the empire (usually Ottoman or Hapsburg) to which the peoples shown on the map belonged before World War 1. They can use history textbooks or historical atlases for assistance. They may also be asked to name the country in which each people lives today. The aim is not to get complete accuracy, but to increase pupils' appreciation of the changing map of Europe and the idea that national states for homogeneous ethnic groups is a relatively new idea in practice.

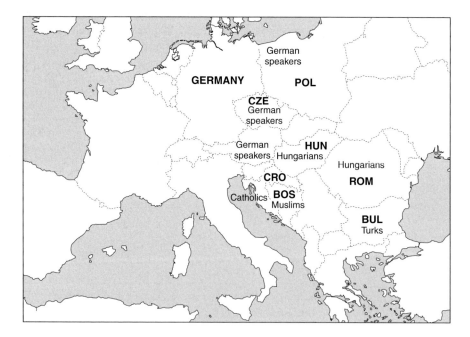

Figure 3b The legacies of multi-national empires in Europe.

The maps shows some language and religious groups in Eastern and Central Europe.

Questions for pupils

1   Can you name the countries in which they are located?
2   Why do you think these groups are located where they are? Compare their location with that of the great multi-national empires of Europe before 1918, especially Austria–Hungary, Ottoman Turkey and Germany.
3   Can you point to connections?

2 *Superpowers*

The map in Figure 3c shows a number of countries that were in the Soviet sphere of influence during the Cold War. Participants can use a current atlas to name some of them and their history texts or an encyclopaedia to say something about the role of the highlighted countries in the struggle between the United States and Soviet Union. This exercise can help with concepts such as 'superpower' and 'sphere of influence'. A similar map could be drawn to illustrate American power around the world in the same period. These maps are especially useful for the USA and USSR as World Superpowers.

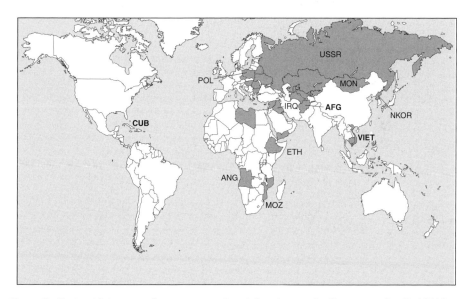

Figure 3c Soviet Union as a Superpower: Russia's sphere of influence in the Cold War.

Questions for pupils

1   Can you name some of the countries on the map that were close allies of the USSR in the Cold War?

2   What important Cold War events occurred in the states marked CUB, VIET and AFG? What implications did they have for the status and reputation of the superpowers?

3 *American states and regions: legacies of the nineteenth century*

This exercise helps learners to understand the concepts of 'the South' and 'the West' in the context of American history. It is suitable for the American history components of the GCSE syllabus, notably Race Relations in the USA and The American West, 1840–95. Pupils are given the map in Figure 3d and the associated questions (which could be set out in a worksheet). They are divided into groups and set to work on the questions. The groups then report to the class as a whole and the teacher clarifies issues that were unresolved. The aim is to convey the idea that elements of nineteenth-century history helped to define the 'West' and the 'South', and that they are not merely defined in geographical terms. The teacher may supplement the questions with others, as long as they bring out the historical identities of the respective regions. Class members can also be encouraged to colour regions on the map or to identify other states.

Figure 3d American states and regions: the legacy of the nineteenth century.

Questions for pupils

1   Can you name the states shown on this map?
2   Which of them belong to the South?
3   Which of them belong to the West?

4   What historical factors helped to bind the South together?
5   How did society in the Western states differ from that in the South in the mid-nineteenth century?
6   The United States acquired CA from a European power. Which one?
7   It acquired NM from a neighbouring country. Which one?
8   It acquired the state of LA from a European power. Which one?
9   Name some important civil rights events that occurred in ARK, AL and MS.

Learning outcomes

On completion of the exercise, class members will be able to: (1) display a deeper knowledge of the countries and regions under study; (2) appreciate the value of maps in academic analysis; (3) evaluate the balance between continuity and change in the state boundaries of Europe or other regions over a particular time period.

Summary

Merits?

☐   Gives life to an otherwise abstract topic.
☐   Visual element encourages interest and participation among class members.
☐   Promotes activity in class.

Possible problems?

☐   Young people's limited knowledge of regional geography.
☐   The approach must be modified when unfamiliar regions are being explored.

Finetuning?

☐   Label maps (country names) to limit impact of gaps in knowledge? This would also have the effect of encouraging pupils to think about particular countries and their mutual relationships, rather than geographical facts. As a rule, the amount of prompting content in the map markers will vary according to the age and prior knowledge of the pupils.

ACTIVITY 26

Collage

Make a montage talk

Description

Setting and context

This activity is ideal as a scene-setter. A History class comes on to a new topic: not an event or a person or a period, but an idea. What is the best way to approach this concept? What is the best way into it? A collage exercise is highly apt.

Learning aims and objectives

The objectives of the exercise are to: (1) help pupils explore a set concept in conventional and non-conventional ways: (2) bring a concept alive through a montage of images; (3) encourage pupils to brainstorm with other pupils.

Resources required

☐ Paper
☐ Glue
☐ A stock of old magazines

Breakdown of method in action

Time needed	Phase of activity
5 mins	Teacher introduces the central concept and explains the activity. Pupils in groups of three are asked to produce collages reflective of the set concept. They can be as imaginative or obscure as they want to be; the only rule is that the images they choose must relate, in some way, to the set concept. They must also be able to explain, and justify, their choice to the rest of the class.
5 mins	In groups of three, the young people are asked to hold a preliminary discussion about the set concept and to exchange initial ideas.
25 mins	Pupils are given paper, glue and a pile of old newspaper sections, magazines and photocopied images. They must produce a provocative, but focused collage.
15 mins	The collages are displayed around the classroom. In sequence, each group introduces its work and explains it to the class. With help from the pupils,

the teacher brings out the main themes in the artwork – and links these ideas to future work and topic areas.

(Total time required = 50 minutes)

Good exemplars

1 *The changing role and status of women*

The source material for this could be the 'Society' sections of newspapers, women's magazines, fashion magazines, especially from the early-to-mid-twentieth century and some from the twenty-first century, as well as photocopies of images from history textbooks. Teachers might help the pupils to organise them in a particular sequence to illustrate change over time. Concepts such as 'feminism' or even 'society' could be introduced via such an exercise.

2 *Impact of science and technology*

Old photographs of familiar landscapes, e.g. in towns or cities, can be helpful here. They could illustrate changing patterns of development or transportation. Another idea might be for pupils to take images of a twenty-first-century urban scene or skyline and cut out or mark features that would not have been there in 1850 (again, modes of transport, skyscrapers, people using mobile phones, street lighting, etc). An understanding of concepts such as 'modernisation' and 'technology' could be developed in this way.

3 *Modern China*

This would rely on old news magazines or newspaper cuttings. Alternatively, pupils could be given current or recent magazines with pictures of capitalist icons in China or young Chinese in Western dress, and then be asked to point to aspects of Chinese life that have changed, either since Maoist times or since Imperial days. Concepts such as modernisation, pragmatism and Communism could be explored in a general way by means of this exercise.

Learning outcomes

Following the activity, pupils will be able to: (1) explore a key concept in a non-conventional manner; (3) appreciate how ideas can be represented in images.

Summary

Merits?

☐ Externalises ideas in a helpful way.
☐ Excellent ice-breaker at the start of a new period of study.
☐ Stimulates spontaneous small-group discussion.
☐ Helps pupils 'see' abstract concepts – and thus breaks down barriers.

Possible problem?

☐ Individuals have got to be selective, careful and thoughtful in the way they locate images and link these images to the set concept; otherwise the exercise becomes meaningless. Thus, pupils have got to be able to justify and explain every image they use.

Finetuning?

☐ Explore two conflicting concepts in the same collage (with either overlapping images or one concept being represented on the left-hand side of the collage and the other on the right)? This could be quite a provocative strategy.

Exploring Dilemmas

Using hard choices to put history in context

Description

Setting and context

Pupils are encouraged to explore the difference between negotiated outcomes and 'just' outcomes by role-playing the scenarios envisaged in the Rawlsian 'veil of igno-rance' metaphor. This exercise employs the metaphor developed by John Rawls to highlight the distinction between what is politically possible and what would be desirable in a perfect outcome. Again, rather than describing the concepts, individ-uals are encouraged to act out Rawlsian games to provoke discussion of their implications. The game could be used to illustrate the dilemmas facing actors involved in domestic public policy-making or to highlight the tensions between negotiated conventions and normative justice in international history.

Learning aims and objectives

The objectives of the exercise are to: (1) help participants explore the constraints on historical actors and the limitations of utopian or principled political agendas; (2) stimulate classroom activity and debate in order to enliven discussion on diffi-cult issues; (3) help pupils explore the common ground between apparently contradictory ideologies or positions.

Resources required

- [ ] Paper
- [ ] Pens
- [ ] A spacious room

Breakdown of method in action

Time needed	Phase of activity
5 mins	Teacher introduces subject matter and outlines aim of session.
10 mins	Learners are asked to take a series of policy decisions or draw up rules for a community in such a way that they could tolerate the outcome, whatever their place in that community. Each pupil works on his/her own list without assistance from others.

10 mins	The group as a whole is invited to discuss a set of rules that would be fair to all players.
10 mins	Individuals are then divided into two groups and asked to consider: (a) how their rules differ from the maximum demands of various groups; and (b) how they would differ from those which might have been negotiated if each person had known his or her role in advance.

(Total time required = 35 minutes)

Good exemplars

1 *Civil Rights in the USA 1865–1980*

Pupils are sitting on a Commission aiming to deal with the root causes of racial conflict in America in the late 1960s. Members of the Commission already agree that discrimination against black Americans and other minorities is wrong and that white violence against blacks must be ended. Beyond this, however, there is disagreement. Some argue that the minorities have suffered so much and for so long that mere equality before the law is not enough. Simply waiting for white communities to treat their fellow citizens with dignity means that nothing happens. Those taking this position argue for busing and for 'positive discrimination'. Others see that approach as replacing one form of discrimination with another, thus weakening the principle of equality itself. They also suggest that America's problems in the late 1960s are not only about racial tensions, but also about a lack of law and order and a disrespect for authority. Pupils debate these issues.

The class is divided into groups. One side takes a position in favour of 'positive discrimination', the other against. Each side puts forward the best arguments for its case. When the debate has covered most of the arguments surrounding the issue, the teacher then asks the groups to reconsider their position, but this time, they are told that they have a hidden identity. This identity will only be revealed after they indicate their preferred solution to the problem of racial conflict in America. Since each group could eventually be named as either black Americans or more cautious whites, they must therefore be more cautious or more moderate in their suggestions. This will illustrate the dilemmas and difficulties surrounding the search for fairness and equality in the area of US race relations in the period after the civil rights years. It helps pupils to explore concepts such as 'justice', 'fairness' and 'discrimination'.

2 *Tories and Liberals in nineteenth-century Britain*

Most of the time pupils focus on the competition between Tories and Liberals in the nineteenth century. This exercise helps them to look for common ground. The class is divided into two groups, one nineteenth-century Liberals, the other Tories.

In the first phase, they debate the merits of Disraeli's Conservatism and Gladstone's Liberal government. This is done under the headings of particular policy areas such as social policy; trade policy; Irish policy; foreign and imperial policy. When all major issues dividing them have been raised, the groups are then told that their party identification is to be changed. However, before their new identities are announced, they must decide on policy positions or suggestions in each of these areas that might appeal to either Disraeli or Gladstone.

3 Napoleon I

The same device can be used to explore the common ground, or apparent common ground, between Napoleon and the French revolutionaries of the late eighteenth century. Pupils are first encouraged to explore the contrasts between Napoleon and the revolutionaries. When these have been exhausted, the class is divided into two groups. They are told that one of the groups will emerge as apologists for Napoleon and the other will eventually be named as a defender of the Revolution and Republic. Before that decision is announced, however, the groups are told to write out five propositions about France and her role in Europe, as well as about foreign monarchies and the rights of citizens. They are reminded that they must design these principles in such a way that they will be able to live with the outcome, whatever the final identity of the group might be. This will force them to be cautious and to write propositions that would appeal to both Napoleon and the revolutionaries. Finally, the class can discuss the question of Napoleon's use of the rhetoric of the Revolution and whether the apparent common ground had any substance. This would help pupils to deepen their understanding of the way in which concepts, such as 'the Rights of Man' or the concept of France's role in Europe, can be used as propaganda tools by different political actors.

Learning outcomes

After the session, learners will be able to: (1) distinguish between 'what is possible' and 'what is desirable'; (2) think critically about how politics and conflicting interests complicate the search for ideal solutions to historical problems.

Summary

Merits?

☐ Problem-solving – classroom activity promotes participation.
☐ Participants are encouraged to go beyond the presentation of their own maximum demands; they must also deal with the needs of others and with constraints on decision-making.

Possible problems?

☐ Decision-making under conditions established by Rawls is particularly difficult, regardless of how well the class is briefed beforehand.

☐ The exercise is more likely to work with older, more able pupils.

☐ Individuals must know the positions or interests of several actors in order to make informed decisions: it will not be sufficient to know one set of arguments.

Finetuning?

☐ The setting – in which learners do not know their role identities in advance – may be difficult to grasp. Thus, teachers may need to spend some time explaining it beforehand and reassuring pupils.

Spatial Mapping

Plot political and historical relationships on a grid

Description

Setting and context

Class members are to define political ideologies or phenomena by plotting them as imaginary variables on a two-dimensional grid. This gives a sense of the important dimensions on which they can be measured, as well as of the nuances in the concepts. When more than one phenomenon is plotted on the same grid, it also shows the relative distances separating them. The purpose of this exercise is to increase individuals' understanding of historical phenomena by evaluating the inter-relationships among key concepts and ideologies. This is done by representing the concepts visually, plotting two scalar variables on perpendicular axes. A good example of an application of this is Robert Dahl's typology of political systems along two axes, one measuring opportunities for political participation; the other, opportunities for political contestation or opposition. Every political system could be given an X and a Y co-ordinate, with a 'pure democracy' scoring highly on both axes (Figure 3f). When applied to the school curriculum, it could be used to examine the personal characteristics of philosophies of key historical figures. Any pair of variables can be used as long as they can be scaled from one extreme to another.

Learning aims and objectives

The objectives of the exercise are to: (1) help pupils to identify relationships among competing ideas or political trends – in particular, to encourage them to debate the relative proximity or distance between differing philosophies or personality types; (2) highlight the importance of scalar concepts, as opposed to rigid dichotomies, in the study of history, without intimidating individuals who might find such concepts difficult to grasp in the abstract; (3) deepen understanding of specific historical personalities or movements of thought.

As with other exercises in this section, the advanced notion of a 'scalar concept' is a useful device for teachers in their preparation of the class. Needless to say, such ideas cannot be raised directly in class. Nonetheless, if the pupils come away from the exercise knowing that the characteristics of various phenomena, individuals or concepts exist *in varying degrees*, the objective of the exercise will have been met.

Resources required

☐ Multiple copies of blank grids like those used in Figure 3f
☐ Pens
☐ Graph paper
☐ Rulers

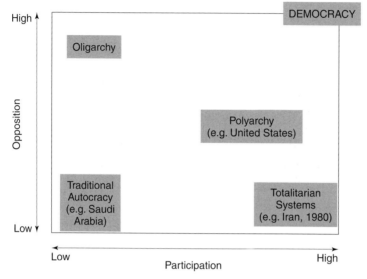

Figure 3f Typologies of political system.[2]

Breakdown of method in action

Time needed	Phase of activity
5 mins	Teacher introduces exercise and explains overall class plan.
5 mins	Pupils broken into groups and blank grids distributed.
5 mins	Teacher describes variables to go on X- and Y-axes.
10 mins	Groups categorise cases (e.g. personalities, countries, political parties, etc) according to their apparent value in each variable.
5 mins	Pupils discuss their judgements about individual cases.
10 mins	Class discuss implications of their classification scheme.

(Total time needed = 40 minutes)

---

2 Derived from R. Dahl, *Polyarchy: Participation and Opposition*, New Haven, Yale University Press, 1971.

Good exemplars

1 *Italian unification*

Camillo Cavour's motives in the process leading to the unification of Italy were quite ambiguous. Was Cavour's policy an instance of Piedmont expansionism, in his own interest, or was it to be seen in the context of the wider Italian nationalism? To what extent was he a pragmatist, simply taking advantage of the initiatives of others, including other Italian nationalists, or an idealist advancing the mid-nineteenth century liberal view of nationalism? Pupils are given grids similar to those in Figure 3g. They are told that the X-axis measures Cavour's position on Piedmont expansionism or Italian nationalism, and the Y-axis shows an assessment of Cavour as pragmatist or idealist. Individuals are asked to place a cross in the central area, indicating which aspects of Cavour are most important. The two groups display their respective grids and justify their decisions. The teacher's role is to help pupils understand the criteria being used to evaluate Cavour. The teacher might also discuss whether Cavour's stance changed over time.

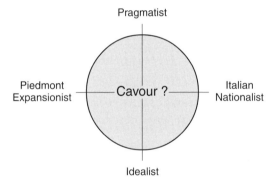

Figure 3g Pinning down Cavour.

2 The Irish Question in the Age of Parnell 1877–1918

This exercise can help pupils to understand the rival movements in Ireland as it moved towards independence. The X-axis could represent a scale ranging from ultra-loyalist to Irish Republican/Nationalist. The Y-axis could represent a scale measuring peaceful or violent methods, a sort of extremism and violence scale. The list of movements whose location is to be plotted might include the Ulster Volunteers, the Irish Republican Brotherhood, Sinn Féin, the Irish Parliamentary Party, the Liberal Party, the Conservative Party. The point of the exercise is to show that there was a range of nuanced positions on both sides, rather than stark distinctions between Unionism and Irish Nationalism. Concepts like Nationalism, Unionism, constitutionalism or extremism can be explored in this way.

3 *Chamberlain and Anglo-German relations in 1918–39*

A similar two-way grid could be used to show the changing prospects for Anglo-German relations 1918–39. The X-axis could represent time. The Y-axis could range from −1 (hostility verging on war) to +1 (peace agreements, appeasement). Pupils could identify key events in this period and plot them on the graph. Munich, for example, would probably represent the highest positive mark on the chart. Even though there would be no objective measure of appeasement or hostility, the attempt to chart the ebb and flow of relations would help pupils to understand the concept of appeasement, but also the fact that there was more than a crude dichotomy (war or appeasement) with many shades of potential conflict and hostility in between. This could be useful for the syllabus component on Chamberlain and Anglo\German Relations.

Learning outcomes

On completion of the exercise, participants will be able to: (1) think about varying degrees of commitment to particular values rather than rigid categories or descriptions; (2) assess relationships among competing ideas; (3) justify their own choices.

Summary

Merits?

☐ Focuses attention on the relative positions of various philosophies and personality types, rather than on absolutes. Pupils are forced to think about scalar concepts.

☐ The potential for disagreement over placement of cases generates discussion and helps class members to see the difficulty associated with efforts to quantify non-numerical variables.

Possible problems?

☐ The exercise depends on prior knowledge of the subject matter under discussion; thus, it may be more suitable for end-of-term summaries or revision than for initial exploration of ideas.

☐ May be difficult to explain to the uninitiated.

Finetuning?

☐ More time could be devoted to explaining the exercise. It is possible to use a dummy run involving typologies of individuals according to easily understood and non-academic phenomena, e.g. music bands rated on sex-appeal and musical ability!

Theory and Practice

Combine discussion and roleplay

Description

Setting and context

This is a relatively simple exercise, which deliberately sets out to combine roleplay sessions and traditional group classes in such a way that they reinforce one another. Many consider reliance on structured or even unstructured class discussion a rather uninteresting approach to the teaching of History. As we know, pupils can sometimes learn more about concepts through roleplay or some other kind of active engagement with the subject. However, on occasions, it is necessary to discuss the core conceptual issues in a conventional way in order for the roleplay to bring them to life. Taken as a whole, the relatively 'serious' discussion and the more relaxed roleplay could be combined to produce more than the sum of their parts. Neither the roundtable discussion nor the roleplay are new in themselves: it is their inter-relationship that reinforces participation and learning among group members.

Learning aims and objectives

The objectives of the exercise are to: (1) reinforce the connections between concepts or documents (which pupils may find 'boring') and the narrative of political and historical conflict with which they are more familiar; (2) encourage pupils to discuss roleplay or other exercises in the context of theoretical or paradigmatic debates and to encourage them to see the connections between the two; (3) provide an integrated context for both the roleplay exercise and the wider class discussion.

Resources required

☐ Case study documents or other reading associated with the set roleplay or simulation exercises
☐ Large conference room
☐ Pencils, pens and paper

Breakdown of method in action

Time needed	Phase of activity
40 mins	'Conventional' class discussion in which pupils present their ideas on concepts that are relevant to understanding of the case study or document.
20 mins	Generalised class discussion on concepts.
10 mins	Break – class members encouraged to continue discussion of concepts.
10 mins	Participants split into groups for roleplay exercise.
30 mins	Negotiation – bargaining aimed at maximising agreement on resolution of the 'problem' posed by the case study.
10 mins	Debriefing.

(Total time needed = 2 hours)

Good exemplars

1 *Peace to War 1918–39*

A roleplay of Stalin and Churchill discussing tactics in dealing with Hitler in the late 1930s. This could be used to explore some aspects of pragmatism in decision-making and the trickier aspects of alliances. In so doing, pupils might realise that alliances are often a matter of convenience as much as principle. In the first phase of the exercise, a group of pupils, representing British officials, advise Churchill on how to approach Stalin. A second group, the Soviet team, advise Stalin. Then there is a period of formal bargaining between them. The second part of the class can look at the idea of alliance-making and at the importance of pragmatism in decision-making. They can also list the conflicting motives of the two sides and examine the consequences for World War II.

2 *USA and USSR as World Superpowers 1945–89*

Teams of Americans and Russians discuss the origins of the Cold War in the period 1940–51. Each side puts its strongest case. In the second half of the class, pupils move out of role and, with the help of the teacher, explore how well-known historical events could be seen so differently. This exercise can help to illustrate the concept of the Cold War and how it was shaped by competing perceptions of history.

3 *The American West 1840–95*

Representatives of native Americans and descendants of the white pioneers meet to discuss the image of the American West that we have today. One side might argue that white settlement and conquest brought the native peoples into the modern world and brought the advantages of democracy. The other will point to the destruction of the native society and the violence and prejudice associated with the conquest. In the second part of the class, pupils might look at how the West was portrayed in movies and the extent to which that has contributed to the adverse situation of native peoples.

Learning outcomes

Following the session, individuals will: (1) have a deeper knowledge of the concepts and historical events under discussion; (2) be able to establish connections between the conceptual issues raised and real historical events.

Summary

Merits?

- [ ] A variety of learning approaches in the same class.
- [ ] Enlivens a standard class through the process of anticipation: the first phase prepares the ground for the second.

Possible problem?

- [ ] Requires long sessions – a minimum of two hours.

Finetuning?

- [ ] It is possible to vary the sequence of the discussion and the roleplay. In some cases, it could be more appropriate to spend more time exploring wider issues and concepts after the roleplay.

ACTIVITY 30   *Suitable for GCSE*

Genealogies

Ideas and their family trees

Description

Setting and context

Family tree structures are used to trace the derivation and evolution of key concepts employed in history. A key task of those teaching history is to get class members to see the historical evolution of key ideas and concepts, as well as their inter-relationship along the way. This exercise encourages pupils to produce the family trees of concepts, showing their original derivation and their connections with related ideas. There is much scope for debate on both of these elements and the exercise should bring this to the fore.

Learning aims and objectives

The objectives of the exercise are to: (1) encourage individuals to trace the history of ideas and concepts and explore connections among and between them; (2) generate class discussion and debate about ideas, concepts and movements in political history.

Resources required

☐ Pens
☐ Drawing paper (large sheets, possible A3 or larger)
☐ History textbooks

Breakdown of method in action

Time needed	Phase of activity
5 mins	Class divided into two groups. Each group starts work on genealogy of concept under discussion.
10 mins	Groups display their 'family trees' and each one justifies its choices.
15 mins	Exchange of views, debate on criteria for placing ideas in a particular sequence or in a particular position relative to others.

5 mins	Discussion of 'root causes' of disagreement among groups and how these conceptual genealogies might affect the real world of politics or political culture.

(Total time needed = 35 mins)

Good exemplars

1 *Germany 1918–39*

A similar evolutionary trail could be traced for the GCSE components on Germany and the two world wars around the concept of *lebensraum* or 'living space', for this cannot be fully understood without reference to Nazi Germany's racial and expansionist policies. These, in turn, require an understanding of concepts such as 'racial superiority', 'militarism' and 'expansionism'.

One pupil's attempt to depict the family tree:

Romantic 19C notions of Germanism and the Germanic race

↓

Wilhelmine notions of *Weltpolitik* etc

↓

Social Darwinism

↓

Post-Versailles frustration

↓

Lebensraum

2 *Social reform 1930–80*

A similar genealogical tree of social reform initiatives could be constructed, running from Poverty and the Poor Law through to the Welfare State. It could be used to link these components of the syllabus.

3 *Race relations in the USA and Africa since 1945*

Looking at how this concept was defined by the US Civil Rights movement, pupils will be drawn to other concepts such as 'race', 'prejudice', 'racism', 'discrimination', 'equality' and 'human rights'. Participants would be encouraged to put approximate dates beside each concept and to organise them in sequence. The object of the

139

exercise is not absolute accuracy, but a sense of movement and direction in the evolution of concepts over time.

Learning outcomes

At the end of the activity, pupils will be able to: (1) display a deeper understanding of the historical context of concepts; (2) critically assess the inter-relationship between values.

Summary

Merits?

☐ The exercise involves activity (formation of groups; construction of genealogies, etc) as opposed to the passive consumption of information.

☐ Group members are alerted to the historical sequences behind the evolution of key concepts.

☐ Pupils are made aware of the multiple meanings assigned to a well-known concept in different historical epochs.

Possible problems?

☐ For those with a strong resistance to concepts, the exercise may not go beyond early phases. The teacher may have to provide support with the more abstract concepts.

☐ This approach requires considerable background knowledge on the part of pupils, e.g. a broad sweep of historical ideas. It could be employed as a tool for the revision and consolidation of material covered over one or two years of study.

Finetuning?

☐ Consideration should be given to the timing of this exercise. It could be run twice: at the beginning of the year to alert pupils to the danger of focusing on a crude chronology of events, and again at the end, as a tool of consolidation. A further advantage of this double run is to show class members how much ground they themselves have covered over the space of the intervening period.

Further reading

R. Dahl, *Polyarchy: Participation and Opposition*, New Haven, Yale University Press, 1971.

G. Davus, *Psychology of Problem Solving: Theory and Practice*, New York, Basic Books, 1973.

C. Dinqwall, *Twentieth Century History Glossary*, NV Entertainment, 1999. Very useful for all levels. The 'terminology' button is particularly helpful for concepts and abstract ideas. Go to: <http://odur.let.rug.nl/~usa/>.

R. Guyver, 'National Curriculum History: Key Concepts and Controversy', *Teaching History*, July 1997.

J. Haenen and H. Schrijnemakers, 'Suffrage, Feudal, Democracy, Treaty ... History's Building Blocks: Learning to Teach Historical Concepts', *Teaching History*, February 2000.

J. Hoefler, 'Critical Thinking and the Use of Optical Illusions', *Political Science and Politics*, 28, 3 September 1994, pp. 538–44.

J. Jenkins, 'Issues in the Teaching of History – Towards a Skills/Concept-led Approach', *Teaching History*, July 1991.

M. Laver, *Playing Politics: The Nightmare Continues*, Oxford, OUP, 1997.

K. Lovell, *An Introduction to Human Development*, London, Macmillan, 1969 (see Chapters 2 and 3 on logical thought and perception).

M. Luckiesh, *Visual Illusions: Their Causes, Characteristics and Applications*, New York, Dover, 1990.

J. Nichol, 'Who wants to Fight? Who wants to Flee? Teaching History from a "Thinking Skills" Perspective', *Teaching History*, May 1999.

J. Scott, 'Contents and Concepts', *Teaching History*, October 1981.

M. Warner, 'Teaching Ideas' site. Additional ideas for teaching about concepts. Go to: <http://www.teachingideas.co.uk/history/contents.htm>.

Review

Concepts are often a source of great anxiety, both for teachers and learners. Teachers worry about finding the appropriate form of words to convey an understanding of a key concept that clarifies it without oversimplification. Moreover, pupils can freeze at the potential difficulty associated with theories and models that are, at first glance, devoid of any concrete reality. Our experience, both in these exercises and in our general teaching, has been that this focus on words is misplaced. We tell our pupils that 'understanding is more important than knowing', but we sometimes ignore this lesson ourselves. Activities which spark the imagination are far more effective than a vain search for words. Once the teacher and the pupil come to a shared understanding of the concept, they can then proceed to develop the appropriate vocabulary with which to commit the ideas to paper.

On the other hand, the exercises described here are not a panacea. There is no guarantee that they will work with all individuals or in all circumstances. It is important to monitor pupil responses and to be flexible. The class might need time to acclimatise itself to the exercise, perhaps using a trial run with material of a non-academic nature on, say, music or sport. Above all else, teachers should pay as much attention to the debriefing period after the class as they do to the conduct of the exercise itself. Even if an activity is disrupted or does not go according to plan, the experience can be used to encourage critical reflection and analysis. The gap between classroom roleplay and real world events is instructive in its own right. Concepts need not be dull. Teachers can and should be creative. After all, Newton did not come to an understanding of gravity by staring at pieces of paper. As teachers, this is a lesson we should learn ourselves before imparting it to our pupils.

Primary Texts

Bringing them alive

Imagination is more important than knowledge.

(*Einstein*)

Introduction

The teaching of history relies on text-based materials. That material can be either a primary text, something that is first-hand evidence, or a secondary source, evidence that is generated after the event. However, to enable pupils and those who teach history to gain most from the subject, and to understand it in a wide-ranging way, primary texts deserve most attention. The ways in which these texts can be interpreted differ; the very interpretation of primary texts can bring new perceptions and ideas into the academic community.

We have chosen ten different ways of teaching and utilising primary texts within the classroom environment. It is all too easy to just run a history class in a tried and tested way, with pupils reading prescribed texts before the class and then a few individuals talking about their interpretation of them during the class. However, if teachers are to be true facilitators of learning, they should be encouraging and actively promoting different means of historical enquiry and different, more inter-active ways of learning. In our ten activities, we have tried to convey the excitement of historical enquiry; in each case we believe that fresh and novel tactics can bring a text alive. We feel that taking an eclectic approach to classroom teaching can foster among pupils an improved understanding of difficult topics and key arguments.[1]

Activities

31 Your Turn Next (Key Stage 3)

32 Questions, Questions (Key Stage 3)

33 Hot-Seating (AS/A-Level)

---

1 The authors would like to acknowledge the contribution of Janet Conneely to this section.

34 Three of a Kind (Key Stage 3)

35 Caption Challenge (GCSE)

36 Graffiti Galore (AS/A-Level)

37 Card Groups (Key Stage 3)

38 Document Drama (GCSE)

39 Blueprint (GCSE)

40 Post-It Wall (Key Stage 3)

The most suitable level for usage is indicated in brackets. However, it should be noted that, with a little adaptation and customisation, many activity ideas contained within this chapter could also be employed at other levels.

ACTIVITY 31

Your Turn Next

Recite and interpret a text – in the round

Description

Setting and context

This activity forms an ideal introduction to a discussion session – a whole-group strategy that can really kick things off in a healthy fashion (and that could also lead on to some kind of mini-group work). It's fast-moving, gets people involved, and puts individuals on the spot! It's a suitable strategy for exploring, and bringing alive, any short, important historical text. And the beauty of this strategy is that everybody in the class is helping everybody else. This activity might not be suitable for all texts – and some might have to be interpreted flexibly.

Learning aims and objectives

The objectives of the exercise are to: (1) familiarise class members with important areas of the text and to challenge them to interpret elements of it spontaneously; (2) increase the 'group' feel of the session; (3) help identify problematic aspects of the text and to raise relevant issues; (4) provoke intra-class discussion.

Resources required

☐ Text
☐ Group of pupils arranged in a circle

Breakdown of method in action

Time needed	Phase of activity
5 mins	Teacher introduces class session and the topic under discussion.
15 mins	Teacher asks Pupil A to read the first line of text out loud; Pupil B (sitting to the left of Pupil A) is invited to comment, query or interpret what he or she has just heard. Pupil C then reads out the second line of text; Pupil D comments and interprets ... and so on until the whole text has been addressed and analysed. (Obviously, the amount of time this activity takes to complete depends on the length of the text under consideration. On the whole this strategy works best with short extracts – an ideal start to a class session).

(Total time needed = 20 minutes)

Good exemplars

1 *The Roman Empire*

Source   *The Roman writer Suetonius records the senators' criticism of Caesar.*[2]

> [1] He accepted excessive honours. [2] He became consul several times and dictator for life. [3] He accepted honours that should only be given to a god: a gold throne, statues beside those of the gods, a special priest, and one of the months of the year was named after him. [4] At the Latin Festival someone placed on his statue a laurel wreath with a white ribbon tied to it (the white ribbon was the sign of a King). [5] The Tribunes gave orders that the ribbon be removed, but Caesar told them off. [6] From that time on he could not get rid of the rumours that he wanted to be King.

[1] Pupil B interprets line read by Pupil A: For example – 'Sounds as if Caesar was corrupt – maybe.'

[2] Pupil D interprets line read by Pupil C: For example – 'According to the author, he was power-crazy, a real obsessive.'

[3] Pupil F interprets line read by Pupil E: For example – 'I think this indicates he had ideas above his station! He was a demi-god, or so he thought!'

[4] Pupil H interprets line read by Pupil G: For example – 'Some people acknowledge his power and influence – in symbolic ways.'

[5] Pupil J interprets line read by Pupil I: For example – 'Not really sure. He wouldn't let anyone question him – he was a real dictator, according to the author of the source.'

[6] Pupil L interprets line read by Pupil K: For example – 'Everyone knew he was power-hungry; his reputation went before him!'

2 *Reformation and religious settlement*

Source   *John Calvin, The Necessity of Reforming the Church (1543)*

> [1] We maintain, then, that at the commencement – when God raised up Luther and others, who held forth a torch to light us into the way of salvation, and who, by their ministry, founded and reared our churches – those heads of doctrine in which the truth of our religion, those in which the pure and legitimate worship of God, and those in which the salvation of men are comprehended, were in a great measure obsolete. [2] We

---

2   The Schools History Project, *Discovering the Past*, London, John Murray, 1991, p. 14.

maintain that the use of the sacraments was in many ways vitiated and polluted. [3] And we maintain that the government of the church was converted into a species of foul and insufferable tyranny. [4] But, perhaps these averments have not force enough to move certain individuals until they are better explained. [5] This, therefore, I will do, not as the subject demands, but as far as my ability will permit. [6] Here, however, I have no intention to review and discuss all our controversies; that would require a long discourse, and this is not the place for it. [7] I wish only to show just how necessary the causes were which forced us to the changes for which we are blamed.

[1] Pupil B interprets line read by Pupil A.

[2] Pupil D interprets line read by Pupil C.

[3] Pupil F interprets line read by Pupil E.

[4] Pupil H interprets line read by Pupil G.

[5] Pupil J interprets line read by Pupil I.

[6] Pupil L interprets line read by Pupil K.

[7] Pupil N interprets line read by Pupil M.

3 *Industrialisation in Britain*

Source   *Cloth manufacturers' petition*

[1] To the Merchants, Clothiers and all such as wish well to the Staple Manufactory of this Nation.

The Humble ADDRESS and PETITION of Thousands, who labour in the Cloth Manufactory

SHEWETH,

That the Scribbling-Machines have thrown thousands of your petitioners out of employ, whereby they are brought into great distress, and are not able to procure a maintenance for their families, and deprived them of the opportunity of bringing up their children to labour: [2] We have therefore to request, that prejudice and self-interest may be laid aside, and that you may pay that attention to the following facts, which the nature of the case requires. [3] The number of Scribbling-Machines extending about seventeen miles south-west of LEEDS, exceed all belief, being no less than one hundred and seventy! And as each machine will do as much work in twelve hours, as ten men can in that time do by hand, (speaking within bounds) and they

> working night and day, one machine will do as much work in one day as would otherwise employ twenty men [4] ... We therefore hope, that the feelings of humanity will lead those who have it in their power to prevent the use of those machines, to give every discouragement they can to what has a tendency so prejudicial to their fellow-creatures [5] ... Many more evils we could enumerate, but we would hope, that the sensible part of mankind, who are not biased by interest, must see the dreadful tendency of their continuance; a depopulation must be the consequence; trade being then lost, the landed interest will have no other satisfaction but that of being last devoured [6] ... Men of common sense must know, that so many machines in use, take the work from the hands employed in Scribbling – and who did that business before machines were invented ... How are those men, thus thrown out of employ to provide for their families?
>
> Signed, in behalf of THOUSANDS, by Joseph Hepworth, Thomas Lobley, Robert Wood, Thos. Blackburn

[1] Pupil B interprets line read by Pupil A

[2] Pupil D interprets line read by Pupil C

[3] Pupil F interprets line read by Pupil E

[4] Pupil H interprets line read by Pupil G

[5] Pupil J interprets line read by Pupil I

[6] Pupil L interprets line read by Pupil K

The schedules for reading and interpreting can, obviously, be varied depending on the number of people in the group and the length and nature of the extract.

Learning outcomes

Following the activity, pupils will be able to: (1) critically assess the main themes in the text; (2) evaluate and interpret the significance of individual lines within the document.

Summary

Merits?

☐ Everybody feels they are contributing to the session – it's communal and democratic.

☐ Puts people on the spot: 'Which line will I get?' 'Which bit will my mate get?'

☐ Pupils are forced to verbalise in front of the whole class – and listen to others.

☐ A nice momentum can develop – it is quite fluent, self-perpetuating and, by necessity, the teacher takes a back seat.

☐ Class members quickly 'get' the idea behind the activity.

☐ Shy individuals don't have to 'compete' with others to make a point.

Possible problems?

☐ Pupils losing their place in the text: 'How long do I read for? Is it up to the next full-stop or that semi-colon?'

☐ Can get tedious – the chosen text must be reasonably short and sweet.

☐ Pressure! Putting individuals on the spot can cause anxiety.

☐ The same people always reading ... and the same people always interpreting. If the text makes its way round the class several times, and if the class contains an even number of pupils, this problem could arise. By popping in and out of the circle, the teacher can preempt this and 'mix things up a bit'.

Finetuning?

☐ Individuals to speak for a set time on their allocated bit of text (not just for as long as they can)?

☐ Throw each bit of text open to the whole group after the allotted pupil has made his or her initial response (or even before).

☐ Pupils could work on the same task in small groups – so as to avoid shy individuals being 'put on the spot' in the big-group context.

ACTIVITY 32

Questions, Questions

Learners quiz learners

Description

Setting and context

A primary text is put under the spotlight. The teacher wants to squeeze as much as possible out of it; and so, class members are asked to devise a set of text-related questions and, at the same time, will be expected to come up with some answers as well.

Learning aims and objectives

The objectives of the exercise are to: (1) focus pupils' minds on a key text; (2) promote a sceptical approach to the document; (3) challenge pupils to think around the source; (4) encourage 'questions' and 'answers'.

Resources required

☐ Copies of the set text (one per pupil)
☐ A set of blank cards

Breakdown of method in action

Time needed	Phase of activity
10 mins	Teacher introduces the set text – and the exercise. Each pupil receives a copy of the document. The class is split into six mini-groups (A–F).
15 mins	Each mini-group studies the text. Debate follows: 'What are the key themes in the text?' 'What issues does it raise?' 'What don't we understand about it?' Each group pins down three questions it would like to ask of another mini-group and writes them on separate cards (e.g. questions could relate to aspects of the text that are difficult to understand, queries, contentious matters that arise from it etc). Group A exchanges questions with Group B; Group C with Group D; and Group E with Group F.
10 mins	Each group explores the questions it has just been given – and jots ideas down on the appropriate card.

| 15 mins | Teacher chairs a big-group plenary, with pupils explaining why they asked the questions they did of other groups and how they respond to the questions that were passed on to them. |

(Total time needed = 50 minutes)

Good exemplars

1 *The Peasants' Revolt (1381)*

Source *Anonimalle Chronicle*

> At this moment the Mayor of London, William Walworth, came up, and the King bade him go to the commons, and make their chieftain come to him. And when he was summoned by the Mayor, by the name of Wat Tighler of Maidstone, he came to the King with great confidence, mounted on a little horse, that the commons might see him . . . And the King said to Walter, 'Why will you not go back to your own country?' . . . Thereupon the said Walter rehearsed the points which were to be demanded; and he asked that there should be no law within the realm save the law of Winchester, and that from henceforth there should be no outlawry in any process of law, and that no lord should have lordship save civilly, and that there should be equality among all people save only the King, and that the goods of Holy Church should not remain in the hands of the religious, nor of parsons and vicars, and other churchmen; but that clergy already in possession should have a sufficient sustenance from the endowments, and the rest of the goods should be divided among the people of the parish.

What kind of questions would pupils ask of other groups when presented with this source?

Possibly:

- [ ] What is distinctive, in general terms, about the Anonimalle Chronicle?
- [ ] What more do we know about Walworth and Tighler?
- [ ] What do you feel is the main message of the text?

2 Revolutions of 1848

Source   *Statement of the Provisional Government (24 February 1848)*

> A reactionary and oligarchical government has just been
> overthrown by the heroism of the people of Paris. That
> government has fled, leaving behind it a trail of blood that
> forbids it ever to retrace its steps. The blood of the people has
> flowed as in July; but this time this noble people shall not be
> deceived. It has won a national and popular government in
> accord with the rights, the progress, and the will of this great and
> generous nation. A provisional government, the result of pressing
> necessity and ratified by the voice of the people and of the
> deputies of the departments, in the session of February 24, is for
> the moment invested with the task of assuring and organising the
> national victory. It is composed of Messieurs Dupont (de
> l'Eure), Lamartine, Cremieux, Arago (of the Institute), Ledru-
> Rollin, Garnier-Pages, Marie, Armand Marrast, Louis Blanc,
> Ferdinand Flocon, and Albert (a workingman). These citizens
> have not hesitated a moment to accept the patriotic commission
> which is imposed upon them by the pressure of necessity. With
> the capital of France on fire, the justification for the present
> provisional government must be sought in the public safety. All
> France will understand this and will lend it the support of its
> patriotism.

What kind of questions would pupils ask of other groups when presented with this
source?

Possibly:

☐ What is the most important thing the extract tells us about the nature of the
Provisional Government?

☐ The words 'patriot' and 'patriotic' are used. What do you feel is the
significance of these terms?

☐ What light does the document shed on the character of 1848 as a
Revolution?

3 *Salahdin and the Crusades*

Source   *Henry II on the Salahdin Tithe (1188)*

1. Each person will give in charity one tenth of his rents and movable goods for the taking of the land of Jerusalem; except for the arms, horses, and clothing of knights, and likewise for the horses, books, clothing, and vestments, and church furniture of the clergy, and except for precious stones belonging to the clergy or the laity.

2. Let the money be collected in every parish in the presence of the parish priest and of the rural dean, and of one Templar and one Hospitaller, and of a servant of the Lord King and a clerk of the King, and of a servant of a baron and his clerk, and the clerk of the bishop; and let the archbishops, bishops, and deans in every parish excommunicate every one who does not pay the lawful tithe, in the presence of, and to the certain knowledge of, those who, as has been said above, ought to be present. And if any one according to the knowledge of those men give less than he should, let there be elected from the parish four or six lawful men, who shall say on oath what is the quality that he ought to have declared; then it shall be reasonable to add to his payment what he failed to give.

3. But the clergy and knights who have taken the cross, shall give none of that tithe except from their own goods and the property of their lord; and whatever their men owe shall be collected for their use by the above and returned intact to them.

What kind of questions would pupils ask of other groups when presented with this source?

Possibly:

☐ Why did the King introduce the Salahdin Tithe?
☐ What do you believe to be the most interesting or controversial aspect of the Salahdin Tithe?
☐ How do you feel it was received by the population at large?

Learning outcomes

At the end of the exercise, pupils will be able to: (1) design a set of relevant and provocative source-related questions; (2) provide balanced responses to a variety of text-related questions; (3) critically evaluate the meaning and significance of the document.

Summary

Merits?

☐ Helps a class to examine and evaluate a text in depth.
☐ Encourages pupils to ask intelligent questions – an underrated skill? – as well as answer them.
☐ Enables pupils to cross-fertilise with others.

Possible problem?

☐ 'Factual' questions being asked by pupils – rather than probing, analytical ones.

Finetuning?

☐ Cards could be passed on to more than just the one group – so that each question receives a variety of responses.
☐ Groups A and B could look at one source; C and D another, and E and F a third.

Hot-Seating

Identify and bring to life a key character

Description

Setting and context

Pick out a character from a key historical text; ask a pupil to act out the part; and thrust him or her into the limelight. For this activity to work well, participants will need substantial preparation time – perhaps a week or two.

Learning aims and objectives

The objectives of the exercise are to: (1) go one step beyond the text itself ... and actually 'pretend' that the main character can be brought alive and interviewed; (2) mix roleplay with textual analysis; (3) encourage learners to think around key historical issues in a creative manner.

Resources required

☐ Text
☐ Movable chairs (so the 'hot-seat' can actually be created)

Breakdown of method in action

Time needed	Phase of activity
5 mins	Introduction – teacher outlines topic under consideration and the mechanics of the 'hot-seating' activity.
10 mins	Pupils are asked to read through text.
5 mins	Big-group discussion: Who are the main characters in the text? Who would it be fascinating to question? Who could reveal important things about related historical debates and controversies? Teacher picks out character in the text for 'hot-seating'.
15 mins	A participant is asked to play the 'hot-seated' figure; the other class members act as question-askers in the 'audience' – they put the hot-seated figure under pressure!

(Total time needed = 35 minutes)

Good exemplars

1 *Nazi Germany*

Source   *Hitler speech (1921)*

> **The Jew** has not grown poorer: he gradually gets bloated, and, if you don't believe me, I would ask you to go to one of our health-resorts; there you will find two sorts of visitors: **the German** who goes there, perhaps for the first time for a long while, to breathe a little fresh air and to recover his health, and the Jew who goes there to lose his fat. And if you go out to our mountains, whom do you find there in fine brand-new yellow boots with splendid rucksacks in which there is generally nothing that would really be of any use? And why are they there? They go up to the hotel, usually no further than the train can take them: where the train stops, they stop too. And then they sit about somewhere within a mile from the hotel, like blow-flies round a corpse.

Which person/s would it be most illuminating to hot-seat? The possibilities are in bold. What questions would the 'audience' ask of the hot-seated figures?

Possibly:

If it's the Jew: 'Why do you feel Hitler is scapegoating you? How are you going to respond?'

If it's the German: 'How aware are you of the Jews in modern Germany? Do you feel they pose a threat to the state?'

2 *The Normans and England 1066–87*

Source   *William of Malmesbury on the Battle of Hastings*

> The **courageous leaders** mutually prepared for battle, each according to his national custom. The **English**, as we have heard, passed the night without sleep, in drinking and singing, and in the morning proceeded without delay against the enemy. All on foot, armed with battle-axes, and covering themselves in front by the juncture of their shields, they formed an impenetrable body which would assuredly have secured their safety that day had not **the Normans**, by a feigned flight, induced them to open their ranks, which till that time, according

> to their custom, had been closely compacted. **King Harold** himself, on foot, stood with **his brothers** near the standard in order that, so long as all shared equal danger, none could think of retreating. This same standard **William** sent, after his victory, to **the Pope**; it was sumptuously embroidered with gold and precious stones, and represented the figure of a man fighting.

Which person/s would it be most illuminating to hot-seat? The possibilities are in bold. What questions would the 'audience' ask of the hot-seated characters?

Possibly:

If it's King Harold: 'How are you feeling in the text? Confident? Frightened? Wary?'

If it's William: 'What is the significance of your standard?'

If it's the Pope: 'What do you make of all this? What is your perspective on the conflict from afar?'

3 Russian Dictatorship 1855–1956

Source   *Count von Moltke on the Coronation of Tsar Alexander II (1855)*

> The sky favored the celebration of the day by the finest weather. At seven in the morning the city was already deserted, for the crowd had flowed to the Kremlin, whose gates were still closed; they opened to us at eight o'clock. We found in Their Majesties' antechamber an army of **gold-embroidered chamberlains,** the **high court functionaries** with their eight-foot-long golden maces, and all the **ladies in the national dress.** The colour of the manteaux is different at different courts – scarlet with gold, silver, blue, amaranth, etc   so that even with the uniform cut there is an agreeable variety in the colours. The headdress is ornamented according to the wealth and taste of the individual – with gold, diamonds, stones, or pearls. The only chair was occupied in turn by **several very old ladies,** who had been standing since seven o'clock, and, from their rich toilets, may have been dressing since four. At nine o'clock the doors of the imperial rooms were opened; the flock of the chamberlains set itself in motion; **the empress-mother** appeared, supported by **her two youngest sons** ... On the previous evening she had assembled **all her children** and blessed them. She was followed by **the hereditary grand duke, the grand dukes** and **grand duchesses, Prince Frederic William, Prince Frederic of the Netherlands, Alexander of Hesse,** and **the other royal princes,** then their suites, and after us the ladies. The procession passed through the halls of Alexander, Vladimir, and George,

> which together make a length of about five hundred feet. On the
> left paraded **the Palace Grenadiers, the Chevalier Guards,
> the Cuirassiers,** with shining breastplates, deputations from the
> other cavalry and infantry regiments – all with standards and
> flags and bright arms ... Behind the troops stood **the bearded
> populace,** with heads uncovered, close together, but without
> crowding.

Which person/s would it be most illuminating to hot-seat? The possibilities are in
bold. What questions would the 'audience' ask of the hot-seated people?

Possibly:

If it's Prince Frederic of the Netherlands: 'What are your relations like with Russia?
How do you feel they will be in the future?'

If it's the Empress's son/s: 'What do you make of all this pomp? How do you feel
your family is feeling in the text?'

If it's the 'bearded populace' (represented by one or several pupils): 'What's your
view of the new Tsar? What are your hopes and expectations?'

Learning outcomes

Following the session, pupils will be able to: (1) identify the key individuals/groups
mentioned in a text; (2) devise a set of source-related questions for the 'hot-
seated' personality; (3) critically review the main issues and controversies that
emerge from a text.

Summary

Merits?

☐ Brings a session alive.
☐ Adds a new dimension to primary text analysis.
☐ Particularly effective where the link between 'text' and 'hot-seated
personality' is brought out in the question-and-answer session.

Possible problems?

☐ Too impromptu? Could lead to fear and anxiety.
☐ Choice of 'actor' – the right kind of person needs to be picked.
☐ An inflexible room – the layout has to change to accommodate the hot-
seating 'event'.

Finetuning?

☐ Do the same thing – but with a week's preparation time.
☐ Do the same thing – but with two or three people in the 'hot seat'.

ACTIVITY 34

Three of a Kind

Simplify a key text – and understand it better

Description

Setting and context

This exercise is all about clarifying a slightly complicated or jargon-filled manifesto or document. It enables pupils to see the text in its true light.

Learning aims and objectives

The objectives of the exercise are to: (1) familiarise pupils with a complex document and make it more accessible; (2) sum up each term of the document in three words (maximum); (3) encourage groupwork and enhance group understanding.

Resources required

☐ Coloured marker pens
☐ Pieces of blank A4 paper
☐ Blu-Tack

Breakdown of method in action

Time needed	Phase of activity
5 mins	Introduction: pupils given particular terms/articles to simplify.
10 mins	Individuals in groups are asked to devise shortened forms (they may have three or four terms/articles to work on).
20 mins	Teacher chairs discussion, with mini-groups in turn revealing their helpful shortened forms, and with other participants noting them down to create a composite list.
10 mins	Debriefing: What do all these shortened forms show? How do they help us understand the document better?

(Total time needed = 45 minutes)

Good exemplars

1 *Chartism*

Source   *The People's Petition (1838)*

> 1. The suffrage to be exempt from the corruption of the wealthy, and the violence of the powerful, must be secret.
> 2. The connection between the representatives and the people, to be beneficial must be intimate.
> 3. With power to choose, and freedom in choosing, the range of our choice must be unrestricted. We are compelled, by the existing laws, to take for our representatives, men who are incapable of appreciating our difficulties, or who have little sympathy with them.

Pupils' ideas
(1) FREE, SECRET ELECTIONS
(2) EFFECTIVE POLITICAL REPRESENTATION
(3) QUALITY MPS REQUIRED

How would these 'answers' provoke discussion?

2 *The United Nations*

Source   *Founding charter*

> Article I
> The purposes of the United Nations are:
>
> 1. To maintain international peace and security, and to that end: to take effective collective measures for the prevention and removal of threats to the peace, and for the suppression of acts of aggression or other breaches of the peace, and to bring about by peaceful means, and in conformity with the principles of justice and international law, adjustment or settlement of international disputes or situations which might lead to a breach of the peace;
> 2. To develop friendly relations among nations based on respect for the principle of equal rights and self-determination of peoples, and to take other appropriate measures to strengthen universal peace;
> 3. To achieve international cooperation in solving international problems of an economic, social, cultural, or humanitarian

> character, and in promoting and encouraging respect for human rights and for fundamental freedoms for all without distinction as to race, sex, language, or religion . . .

Pupils' ideas
Article I
(1) COLLECTIVE PEACE AIM
(2) FRIENDLY INTERNATIONAL COMMUNITY
(3) JOINT PROBLEM SOLVING

How would these 'answers' provoke discussion?

3 *World War II*

Source *Potsdam Protocol (August 1945)*

> 1. There shall be established a Council composed of the Foreign Ministers of the United Kingdom, the Union of Soviet Socialist Republics, China, France, and the United States.
> 2. The Council shall normally meet in London which shall be the permanent seat of the joint Secretariat which the Council will form. Each of the Foreign Ministers will be accompanied by a high-ranking Deputy, duly authorized to carry on the work of the Council in the absence of his Foreign Ministers, and by a small staff of technical advisers.
> 3. The first meeting of the Council shall be held in London not later than September 1st 1945. Meetings may be held by common agreement in other capitals as may be agreed from time to time.

Pupils' ideas
(1) NEW COUNCIL ESTABLISHED
(2) LONDON – MAIN CENTRE
(3) IMMEDIATE MEETING REQUIRED

How would these 'answers' provoke discussion?

Learning outcomes

At the end of the exercise, participants will be able to: (1) understand and evaluate a key historical document (as a whole and via its individual terms); (2) critically assess the thinking and rationale behind a document.

Summary

Merits?

- [ ] It's fun, enjoyable, and makes 'difficult' documents accessible.
- [ ] Confronts pupils with a specific challenge.
- [ ] Deformalises the classroom atmosphere.
- [ ] Focuses pupils' minds.
- [ ] Contains elements of competition and teamwork.
- [ ] Individuals know what is required and they 'get' the gist of the exercise.

Possible problems?

- [ ] Over-simplification: the aim is to simplify (and then build upon this), not to over-simplify in a way that would not be helpful or appropriate.
- [ ] 'Three words' or 'a three-word sentence'?

Finetuning?

- [ ] How about asking class members for five-word summaries?
- [ ] Ask two groups to work on the same articles – and then compare and contrast their efforts.

ACTIVITY 35

Caption Challenge

Attach headlines to texts

Description

Setting and context

Sometimes teachers want to examine every nuance of a primary document; at other times, however, all they want to do is get a sense of the gist or the general message of a text. This activity is extremely appropriate when the latter is the case.

Learning aims and objectives

The objectives of the exercise are to: (1) bring a fresh approach to textual analysis; (2) appraise documents from a variety of perspectives; (3) compare and contrast set texts.

Resources required

☐ Copies of the text/texts to be analysed
☐ Coloured marker pens
☐ Poster-sized paper
☐ Blu-Tack

Breakdown of method in action

Time needed	Phase of activity
15 mins	The class is divided into mini-groups. The mini-groups are given different texts to focus on and explore. The teacher asks for two captions per text: one that reflects the pupils' interpretation of the text, and another that would be representative of how the author feels. Following the discussion, the teacher asks each group to write up their captions on poster-size paper.
10 mins	The groups' captions are fixed to the wall and then introduced and explained. A big-group discussion can follow: What are the strengths and weaknesses of each caption? What historical issues do they highlight? How could they be improved?

(Total time needed = 25 minutes)

Good exemplars

1 *Chartism*

Source   *People's Charter (1837)[3]*

> Unto the Honourable the Commons of the United Kingdom of
> Great Britain and Ireland in Parliament assembled, the Petition
> of the undersigned, their suffering countrymen. HUMBLY
> SHEWETH, That we, your petitions, dwell in a land whose
> merchants are noted for enterprise, whose manufacturers are
> very skilful, and whose workmen are proverbial for their
> industry. The land itself is goodly, the soil rich, and the
> temperature wholesome; it is abundantly furnished with the
> materials of commerce and trade; it has numerous and
> convenient harbours; in facility of internal communication it
> exceeds all others. For three-and-twenty years we have enjoyed a
> profound peace. Yet, with all these elements of national
> prosperity, and with every disposition and capacity to take
> advantage of them, we find ourselves overwhelmed with public
> and private suffering. We are bowed down under a load of taxes;
> which, notwithstanding, fall greatly short of the wants of our
> rulers; our traders are trembling on the verge of bankruptcy; our
> workmen are starving; capital brings no profit, and labour no
> remuneration; the home of the artificer is desolate, and the
> warehouse of the pawnbroker is full; the workhouse is crowded,
> and the manufactory is deserted. We have looked on every side,
> we have searched diligently in order to find out the causes of a
> distress so sore and so long continued. We can discover none in
> nature, or in Providence.

What headlines would the pupils attach to the document?

From the author's perspective:

WHY US?

or

TAXED TO DEATH

or

WHEN WILL THIS SUFFERING END?

---

3   *The Life and Struggles of William Lovett*, New York, Knopf, 1920, pp. 478–482.

From the pupils' perspective:

PETITIONERS' PLEA

or

THEY THINK IT'S ALL OVER ...

or

CHARTER ROCKS BRITAIN

How would these captions provoke discussion?

2 USA and USSR as World Superpowers 1945–89

Source   *Winston Churchill, 'Iron Curtain Speech' (1946)*

I have a strong admiration and regard for the valiant Russian people and for my wartime comrade, Marshal Stalin. There is deep sympathy and goodwill in Britain – and I doubt not here also – toward the peoples of all the Russias and a resolve to persevere through many differences and rebuffs in establishing lasting friendships. It is my duty, however, to place before you certain facts about the present position in Europe. From Stettin in the Baltic to Trieste in the Adriatic an iron curtain has descended across the Continent. Behind that line lie all the capitals of the ancient states of Central and Eastern Europe. Warsaw, Berlin, Prague, Vienna, Budapest, Belgrade, Bucharest and Sofia; all these famous cities and the populations around them lie in what I must call the Soviet sphere, and all are subject, in one form or another, not only to Soviet influence but to a very high and in some cases increasing measure of control from Moscow. The safety of the world, ladies and gentlemen, requires a unity in Europe, from which no nation should be permanently outcast. It is from the quarrels of the strong parent races in Europe that the world wars we have witnessed, or which occurred in former times, have sprung. Twice the United States has had to send several millions of its young men across the Atlantic to fight the wars. But now we all can find any nation, wherever it may dwell, between dusk and dawn. Surely we should work with conscious purpose for a grand pacification of Europe within the structure of the United Nations and in accordance with our Charter. In a great number of countries, far from the Russian frontiers and throughout the world, Communist fifth columns are established and work in complete unity and absolute obedience to the directions they receive from the Communist centre.

What headlines would the pupils attach to the document?

From the author's perspective:

POST-WAR PARALYSIS LOOMS

or

I ADMIRE THE SOVIETS BUT …

or

CURTAINS TO A UNITED EUROPE!

From the pupils' perspective:

CHURCHILL – UN IS THE KEY

or

OPPORTUNITY KNOCKS FOR WEST

or

CHURCHILL BLASTS COMMUNIST FIFTH COLUMNS

How would these captions provoke discussion?

3 *The Role and status of women in Britain 1880–1945*

Source   *Caroline Norton, English Laws for Women in the Nineteenth Century (1845)*

And now let me ask, is there any reason why attention should not be called to the defective state of Laws for Women in England, as attention has been called to other subjects – namely, by individual effort? Is there any reason why (attention being so called to the subject) women alone, of the more helpless classes, the classes set apart as not having free control of their own destinies, should be denied the protection which in other cases supplies and balances such absence of free control? Are we to believe that the gentlemen of Great Britain are so jealous of their privilege of irresponsible power in this one respect, that they would rather know redress impossible in cases which they themselves admit to be instances of the grossest cruelty and baseness, than frame laws of control for themselves such as they are willing to frame for others?

What headlines would the pupils attach to the document?

From the author's perspective:

THE LAW IS AN ASS!

or

PROTECTION IS PRIORITY

or

WE ARE HELPLESS!

From the pupils' perspective:

NORTON LAYS LAW DOWN

or

BRITISH MEN AND THEIR 'IRRESPONSIBLE POWER'

or

SEX WAR LOOMS

How would these captions provoke discussion?

Learning outcomes

Following the exercise, pupils will be able to: (1) display an awareness of the meaning of key historical texts; (2) assess a document from a range of perspectives; (3) critically review the suitability of various newspaper headlines.

Summary

Merits?

☐ Helps individuals think through the real importance of historical texts.
☐ Demands clarity and accuracy.
☐ Brings a subject alive – historical topics are given a modern media 'makeover'.
☐ Encourages pupils to be clinical in the way they dissect a text.
☐ Enables pupils to view texts from different angles.

Possible problem?

☐ The danger of over-simplification.

Finetuning?

☐ The pupils could be asked to caption texts for different newspapers with different political outlooks.
☐ Ask participants to produce a Ceefax-style precis rather than a headline.

ACTIVITY 36

Graffiti Galore

Deconstruct a passage

Description

Setting and context

This activity is ideal when the attention of a History class turns to one short and particularly important or profound passage of text.

Learning aims and objectives

To help pupils unlock the meaning of, and nuances within, a set passage.

Resources required

- ☐ Poster-sized paper
- ☐ Coloured marker pens
- ☐ Blu-Tack

Breakdown of method in action

Time needed	Phase of activity
5 mins	The teacher reveals a key quotation that needs examining. He or she writes this short passage up in giant letters on a piece of poster-size paper – and puts it up on the classroom wall.
10 mins	In turn, group members pick up a marker pen and highlight just one aspect of the quote that is of particular interest or significance. They might add a single word, a phrase, a piece of grammar or punctuation, or maybe even a connection between two or three different aspects of the quote (participants can circle key terms or use arrows to make links). When they have added their own little bit of graffiti to the quotation, each person has to explain what they've done and why they've done it.
10 mins	The teacher chairs a plenary-style discussion that focuses on the main issues to come out of the session. How, and in what ways, has the quotation come alive?

(Total time needed = 25 minutes)

Good exemplars

1 *The Crusades*

Source   *The chronicler Fulcher of Chartres*

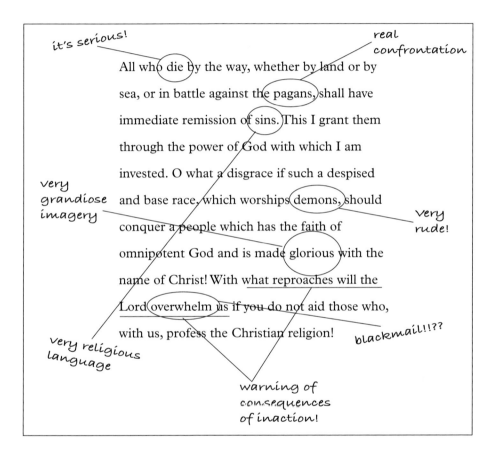

What kind of discussion would this graffiti provoke?

2 *German unification*

Source   *Bismarck on Austria*

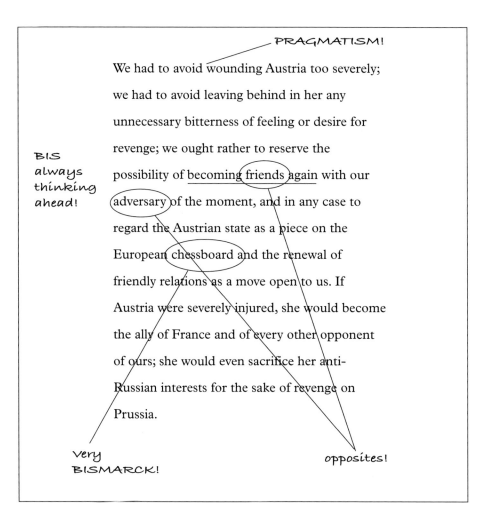

What kind of discussion would this graffiti provoke?

3 Napoleon I

Source   *The Emperor speaks in April 1814 after his failed invasion of Russia and defeat by the Allies*

---

very formal!

Soldiers of my Old Guard: I bid you farewell.

For twenty years I have constantly accompanied

you on the road to (honour and glory.) These latter *VAIN!!!*

times, as in the days of our prosperity, you have

invariably been models of courage and fidelity.

With men such as you our cause could not be

lost; but the war would have been interminable;

it would have been civil war, and that would

have entailed deeper misfortunes on France. I

have sacrificed all of my interests to those of the

martyrdom!
patriotism! country. I go, but you, my friends, will continue *early*
nationalism
to serve France. Her happiness was my only

thought. It will still be the object of my wishes.

Do not regret my fate; if I have consented to

survive, it is to serve your glory. I intend to write

the history of the great achievements we have

performed together. Adieu, my friends. Would I

could press you all to my heart.

Napoleon the soldier
praising soldiers

inevitable?   *emotion —*
                                              finally.

What kind of discussion would this graffiti provoke?

These passages would be written up in giant-size letters. Pupils would be invited to add graffiti to them in line with their thoughts – see above!

Learning outcomes

At the end of the session, class members will be able to: (1) review the main themes in a passage; (2) analyse the linguistic nuances in a text; (3) assess the overall meaning and significance of a document.

Summary

Merits?

- [ ] Focuses learners' minds.
- [ ] The exercise is visual – and individuals will remember it.
- [ ] Changes the classroom atmosphere.
- [ ] Many unexpected outcomes can emerge.

Possible problem?

- [ ] Large, general points being made – rather than narrow, specific ones.

Finetuning?

- [ ] Different coloured marker pens: if each person uses a different colour the points being made would stand out more.

ACTIVITY 37

Card Groups

Give pupils a special task

Description

Setting and context

This classroom technique is simple and effective. When the teacher wants to thoroughly dissect one key text in a session, it is ideal!

Learning aims and objectives

The objectives of the exercise are to: (1) promote greater understanding of a key primary text; (2) involve pupils in all aspects of classroom analysis; (3) encourage pupils to share their ideas with others.

Resources required

☐ Cards with key questions.

Breakdown of method in action

Time needed	Phase of activity
5 mins	Teacher introduces the text to be considered and splits the class into three mini-groups and hands each a card with a key question relating to the text.
5 mins	Teacher stands up and reads the text out aloud. While the teacher is reading, the mini-groups are asked to focus on and think about their question.
15 mins	Having become familiar with the text, each mini-group sits down to discuss its question. Their task is to reach some preliminary conclusions about the question in hand.
15 mins	New 'randomised' groups are formed. This means that each new group contains a mixture of people (who would have been focused on different questions in the first phase of groupwork). They put all their ideas about the text together and arrive at some general conclusions.
10 mins	Teacher chairs a big-group plenary discussion. After all the small-group discussion, what general themes emerge from the text?

(Total time needed = 50 minutes)

Good exemplars

1 *Joan of Arc*

Source   *Report of her trial (1431)*

> Again asked whether she confessed her sins each year: she answered yes, to her own curé; and when the curé was hindered she with his permission confessed to another priest. Sometimes also, twice or thrice as she believed, she confessed to the friars. And this was in the said town of Neufchâteau. And she had been in the habit of receiving the Eucharist at Easter. Asked whether she had been in the habit of receiving the Sacrament of the Eucharist at any other feasts save Easter: she told her questioner to pass on. She further confessed that when she was thirteen years old she had a voice from God to aid her in self-discipline. And the first time she was greatly afraid. And this voice came about noon in summer in her father's garden, and she had fasted the day before. And she heard the voice on her right hand toward the church, and she seldom heard it without a light. Which light comes from the same side as the voice, but is usually great. And when she came to France she often heard this voice. Asked how she saw the light which she said was there present when it was on one side; to this she answered nothing, but passed to other things. She moreover said that if she were in a grove she distinctly heard voices coming to her. She also said that the voice seemed to her worthy, and she believes that it was sent by God; and after she had heard it three times she knew that it was the voice of an angel. She also said that it always guarded her well, and that she knew it well.

Phase I of Groupwork

Question for Group A: What kind of general picture do we get of the trial?

Question for Group B: How does Joan come across in the text?

Question for Group C: How genuine are Joan's religious convictions?

Phase II of Groupwork

Each new group contains:

One member of Group A

One member of Group B

One member of Group C

The discussion question for each new group is: What general themes emerge from this document and what is its overall significance and importance?

2 *The Holocaust*

Source   *Wannsee Protocol (20 January 1942)*

> At the beginning of the discussion Chief of the Security Police and of the SD, SS-Obergruppenführer Heydrich, reported that the Reich Marshal had appointed him delegate for the preparations for the final solution of the Jewish question in Europe and pointed out that this discussion had been called for the purpose of clarifying fundamental questions ... The Chief of the Security Police and the SD then gave a short report of the struggle which has been carried on thus far against this enemy, the essential points being the following:
>
>   a) the expulsion of the Jews from every sphere of life of the German people,
>
>   b) the expulsion of the Jews from the living space of the German people.
>
>   In carrying out these efforts, an increased and planned acceleration of the emigration of the Jews from Reich territory was started, as the only possible present solution.

Phase I of Groupwork

Question for Group A: What is the background to the Wannsee Protocol?

Question for Group B: What do you feel are the key parts of the text?

Question for Group C: If you were a Jew, what would be your immediate reaction to it?

Phase II of Groupwork

Each new group contains:

One member of Group A

One member of Group B

One member of Group C

The discussion question for each new group is: What general themes emerge from this document and what is its overall significance and importance?

3 *The Domesday Book*

Source   *The Anglo-Saxon Chronicle (1086) on the genesis of the survey*

> The King spent Christmas with his councillors at Gloucester, and held his court there for five days, which was followed by a three-day synod held by the Archbishop and the clergy. At this synod Maurice was elected Bishop of London and William Bishop of Norfolk and Robert Bishop of Cheshire: they were all chaplains of the King. After this the King ... sent his men all over England into every shire to ascertain how many hundreds of 'hides' of land there were in each shire. He also had it recorded how much land his archbishops had, and his diocesan bishops, his abbots and his earls, and – though I may be going into too great detail – and what or how much each man who was a landholder here in England had in land or live-stock, and how much money it was worth. So very thoroughly did he have the inquiry carried out that there was not a single 'hide,' not one virgate of land, not even – it is shameful to record it, but it did not seem shameful for him to do – not even one ox, nor one cow, nor one pig which escaped notice in his survey.

Phase I of Groupwork

Question for Group A: What is a synod?

Question for Group B: What is a hide?

Question for Group C: What do you feel are the key elements of the text?

Phase II of Groupwork

Each new group contains:

One member of Group A

One member of Group B

One member of Group C

The discussion question for each new group is: What general themes emerge from this document and what is its overall significance and importance?

Learning outcomes

At the end of the session, individuals will be able to: (1) review the text from one specific perspective; (2) refer to other groups' findings and ideas in their overall evaluation of the document; (3) critically assess the main themes in, and the overall significance of, the source.

Summary

Merits?

- ☐ Gives pupils a specific task.
- ☐ Enables them to cross-fertilise with other class members.
- ☐ Fast-moving.
- ☐ Involves both small-group and big-group discussion.

Potential problem?

- ☐ In the first phase of groupwork, pupils have got to be disciplined: they shouldn't let their small-group discussion go beyond the confines of their specific question.

Finetuning?

- ☐ This activity would also be effective, in exactly the same way, if the source under consideration wasn't a text, but a poster, cartoon or an image of a different kind.

ACTIVITY 38

Document Drama

Act out an extract

Description

Setting and context

Drama can be a stimulating and interesting experience. It is a device that lends itself to larger classes and can be used to build up pupils' confidence. Pupils are asked to take on the role of key characters from within the text. They are then challenged to act out that role within the class session.

Learning aims and objectives

The objectives of the exercise are to: (1) appraise a text in a non-conventional manner; (2) improve pupils' understanding of difficult historical concepts; (3) promote deep understanding of issues and themes in the text.

Resources required

☐ Appropriate primary source readings to be read at the start of the session.

Breakdown of method in action

Time needed	Phase of activity
5 mins	Teacher outlines the aims and focus of the session.
10 mins	Class members read a key primary source document. They are asked to identify the main characters in the text.
25 mins	Pupils are given characters 'to play'. Ideally, two or three people are asked to take responsibility for one character. The teacher then asks questions of the 'characters'. He or she might say: 'How do you feel you are portrayed in the text?' Each group of pupils is given a few minutes to discuss and formulate its response. The teacher then asks each group to report back with its thoughts. After this, the teacher asks another provocative question of the roleplay groups: 'As X or Y, how do you view the other people mentioned in this text?' The groups spend another few minutes discussing this question – and then report back. This process goes on until four or five questions have been debated. Hopefully too, the roleplay groups will

start questioning each other – in addition to answering the set questions
from the teacher.

10 mins	Debriefing session with pupils out of role. The teacher asks questions such as: 'So, what themes came out of that session?' 'How do you feel the characters in the text relate to each other?' 'In the light of our drama, how should we look upon the primary source?' 'Do you feel you've now got an enhanced understanding of the text?'

(Total time needed = 50 minutes)

Good exemplars

1 World War II

Source   *Neville Chamberlain, Peace in Our Time (30 September 1938)*

> We, the **German Führer and Chancellor**, and the **British Prime Minister**, have had a further meeting today and are agreed in recognising that the question of Anglo-German relations is of the first importance for two countries and for Europe. We regard the agreement signed last night and the Anglo-German Naval Agreement as symbolic of the desire of **our two peoples** never to go to war with one another again. We are resolved that the method of consultation shall be the method adopted to deal with any other questions that may concern our two countries, and we are determined to continue our efforts to remove possible sources of difference, and thus to contribute to assure the peace of Europe … my good friends this is the second time in our history that there has come back from Germany to Downing Street peace with honour. I believe it is peace in our time.

2 Russia 1917–41

Source   *Abdication of Nikolai II (15 March 1917)*

> By the Grace of God, We, **Nikolai II, Emperor of All the Russias, Tsar of Poland, Grand Duke of Finland, and so forth**, to all our faithful subjects be it known: In the days of a great struggle against **a foreign enemy** who has been endeavouring for three years to enslave our country, it pleased God to send Russia a further painful trial. Internal troubles threatened to have a fatal effect on the further progress of this

> obstinate war. The destinies of Russia, the honour of **her heroic Army**, the happiness of **the people**, and the whole future of our beloved country demand that the war should be conducted at all costs to a victorious end. The cruel enemy is making his last efforts and the moment is near when our valiant Army, in concert with **our glorious Allies**, will finally overthrow the enemy. In these decisive days in the life of Russia we have thought that we owed to our people the close union and organisation of all its forces for the realisation of a rapid victory; for which reason, in agreement with **the Imperial Duma**, we have recognised that it is for the good of the country that we should abdicate the Crown of the Russian State and lay down the Supreme Power. Not wishing to separate ourselves from our beloved son, we bequeath our heritage to our brother, **the Grand Duke Mikhail Alexandrovich**, with our blessing for the future of the Throne of the Russian State.

3 USA 1918–41

Source   *Franklin D. Roosevelt, First Inaugural (4 March 1933)*

> I am certain that **my fellow Americans** expect that on my induction into the Presidency I will address them with a candor and a decision which the present situation of our Nation impels ... Values have shrunken to fantastic levels; taxes have risen; our ability to pay has fallen; government of all kinds is faced by serious curtailment of income; the means of exchange are frozen in the currents of trade; the withered leaves of industrial enterprise lie on every side; **farmers** find no markets for their produce; the savings of many years in **thousands of families** are gone. More important, a host of **unemployed citizens** face the grim problem of existence, and an equally great number toil with little return ... Practices of **the unscrupulous money changers** stand indicted in the court of public opinion, rejected by the hearts and minds of men.

In each extract, the possible roleplay groups are indicated in bold. The author of each extract (Chamberlain, Nikolai II and Roosevelt) could also take his place in the roleplay. Pupils need to engage in extensive reading and general preparation before they can be asked to take part in such a session.

Learning outcomes

On completion of the exercise, group members will be able to: (1) assess the nature and significance of the document; (2) critically review the relationship between the text and the individuals/groups that feature in it; (3) evaluate the merits of roleplay as an aid to historical understanding.

Summary

Merits?

- ☐ Drama allows everyone in the class to contribute.
- ☐ Brings the text alive – literally!
- ☐ Encourages individuals to work as part of a small group and to discuss their roles and their attitude to the other roleplay characters.

Possible problems?

- ☐ Shyness might prevent some pupils from fully entering into the spirit of the activity – but working in a group, and not as individuals, should help them.
- ☐ Roleplay might be viewed by some as not rigorous enough. The teacher's role, however, is to dispel any such notions!

Finetuning?

- ☐ The mini-groups could be given focused questionnaires to answer 'in role' – instead, or in addition to, answering the teacher's questions.

ACTIVITY 39

Blueprint

From first principles devise a text

Description

Setting and context

Turn a typical text-based session on its head. Instead of just looking at a charter, or manifesto, or whatever, ask pupils to create their own blueprint. Reveal the 'real' version at the end of the class, and then compare and contrast ...

Learning aims and objectives

The objectives of the exercise are to: (1) place the classroom onus on pupils and make them think creatively and imaginatively; (2) approach a historical text from a different kind of direction; (3) provoke group members by making them compete – who can get closest to the real text?

Resources required

☐ Paper
☐ Coloured marker pens
☐ Blu-Tack

Breakdown of method in action

Time needed	Phase of activity
5 mins	Teacher introduces session and gives pupils a flavour of the charter or manifesto under consideration.
20 mins	The onus is shifted to the young people, working in groups. They are asked to 'create' the charter or manifesto from scratch (and to base their thinking around ideas and principles outlined in other classes).
10 mins	The mini-groups pin their efforts to the wall. The teacher reads out, or passes round copies of, the real one ... and then chairs a discussion about the exercise and what has emerged from it – focusing in particular on the similarities and differences evident between the 'real' and 'imagined' documents.

(Total time needed = 35 minutes)

Good exemplars

1 *World War I*

Source   *Wilson's Fourteen Points (January 1918)*

President Wilson addresses the twin questions of why war broke out and how another war could be avoided. What 'Fourteen Points' would pupils come up with if, in January 1918, they had been put in Wilson's position? How would these compare with the 'real' Fourteen Points?

Pupils' efforts:

(1)   DISARMAMENT OF SOME KIND.

(2)   INTERNATIONAL COOPERATION IN THE BALKANS.

(3)   SELF-DETERMINATION FOR ETHNIC GROUPS THAT WANT IT

... etc, etc.

The 'real' Fourteen Points (to be revealed after the pupils have produced their version):

1. Diplomacy shall be open.
2. Freedom of navigation on the seas.
3. The removal of economic barriers.
4. The reduction of armaments.
5. The settlement of colonial problems with reference to the interest of colonial peoples.
6. The evacuation of Russia. Goodwill towards her.
7. The restoration of Belgium.
8. The restoration of France and her recovery of Alsace–Lorraine.
9. Italian frontiers along lines of nationality.
10. Autonomous development for the peoples of Austria–Hungary.
11. Territorial integrity for the Balkan states.
12. Free passage through the Dardanelles and autonomous development for the peoples of the Turkish Empire.
13. An independent Poland.
14. An association of nations.[4]

How would the 'real' and 'imagined' documents provoke discussion?

---

4   J. Watson, *Success in Twentieth Century World Affairs*, London, John Murray, 1974, pp. 33–4.

2 *World War II*

Source   *The Nazi–Soviet Non-aggression Pact (1939)*

The Nazi–Soviet Pact contains a preamble and seven main articles. If pupils were asked to prepare the treaty, in the circumstances of 1939, as Nazi and Soviet officials, what kind of preamble and what kind of articles would they come up with?

Pupils' efforts:

CIRCUMSTANCES HAVE FORCED US INTO THIS ALLIANCE, BUT IT HAS REAL MEANING AND SIGNIFICANCE FOR BOTH STATES.

(1)   THE TREATY IS BEING SIGNED FOR MUTUAL SELF-INTEREST.

(2)   OUR TWO COUNTRIES WILL SHARE INTELLIGENCE.

(3)   THE PACT WILL RUN INDEFINITELY UNTIL ONE PARTY WISHES TO TERMINATE IT.

... etc, etc.

The 'real' Nazi–Soviet Pact (to be revealed after the pupils have produced their version):

> The Government of the German Reich and The Government of the Union of Soviet Socialist Republics desirous of strengthening the cause of peace between Germany and the USSR, and proceeding from the fundamental provisions of the Neutrality Agreement concluded in April, 1926 between Germany and the USSR, have reached the following Agreement:
>
> Article I. Both High Contracting Parties obligate themselves to desist from any act of violence, any aggressive action, and any attack on each other, either individually or jointly with other Powers.
>
> Article II. Should one of the High Contracting Parties become the object of belligerent action by a third Power, the other High Contracting Party shall in no manner lend its support to this third Power.
>
> Article III. The governments of the two High Contracting Parties shall in the future maintain continual contact with one another for the purpose of consultation in order to exchange information on problems affecting their common interests.

How would the 'real' and 'imagined' documents provoke discussion?

3 *Russia 1917–41*

Source *The April Theses (April 1917)*

In the first six points, Lenin addresses a range of issues: the war, the post-February situation in Russia, the Provisional Government, the Soviets, the notion of a parliamentary republic and the agrarian issue. What 'Theses' would pupils come up with if, in April 1917, they had been placed in Lenin's position? How would these compare with the 'real' April Theses?

Pupils' efforts:

(1)   WE MUST END THE WAR THAT IS RUINING THE COUNTRY.

(2)   SOMETHING MUST BE DONE TO SORT OUT THE LAND PROBLEM.

(3)   THE PROVISIONAL GOVERNMENT IS A BOURGEOIS EVIL.

… etc, etc.

The 'real' April Theses (to be revealed after the pupils have produced their version):

> 1. In our attitude towards the war not the slightest concession must be made to 'revolutionary defencism', for under the new government of Lvov & Co., owing to the capitalist nature of this government, the war on Russia's part remains a predatory imperialist war.
> 2. The peculiarity of the present situation in Russia is that it represents a transition from the first stage of the revolution – which, because of the inadequate organisation and insufficient class-consciousness of the proletariat, led to the assumption of power by the bourgeoisie – to its second stage which is to place power in the hands of the proletariat and the poorest strata of the peasantry …
> 3. No support to the Provisional Government; exposure of the utter falsity of all its promises, particularly those relating to the renunciation of annexations. Unmasking, instead of admitting, the illusion-breeding 'demand' that this government, a government of capitalists, should cease to be imperialistic …

How would the 'real' and 'imagined' documents provoke discussion?

Learning outcomes

At the end of the activity, group members will be able to: (1) devise their own version of a text on the basis of their own knowledge and insight; (2) critically review a variety of source-related issues; (3) compare and contrast the 'real' document and their own version.

Summary

Merits?

- [ ] Puts the onus on individuals.
- [ ] A healthy element of competition between groups.
- [ ] Makes pupils think about an issue from first principles.
- [ ] An interesting 'compare and contrast' element (e.g. comparing pupils' efforts with the 'real' text).
- [ ] Fosters empathy.
- [ ] Focuses individuals' minds on a definite 'challenge'.

Possible problems?

- [ ] A daunting task – pupils need to be reassured.
- [ ] Over-large sub-groups – there should be a maximum of two or three individuals in each group, so as to avoid a situation where 'too many cooks spoil the broth'.
- [ ] Is there a 'right answer'? There is – obviously – but the aim of the session is just to get as close as possible to the main themes in the document.

Finetuning?

- [ ] The teacher to explain the complexity of the task right at the start – so that the pupils aren't dominated by the task of getting the charter terms 'spot on'.
- [ ] Ask pupils to do the same task, but from different political perspectives.

ACTIVITY 40   *Suitable for Key Stage 3*

Post-It Wall

Deconstruct a text – and display the key words

Description

Setting and context

This technique is ideal for any classroom situation in which the teacher wants to encourage a simple form of textual analysis. This activity has many variations and can be adapted in several different ways.

Learning aims and objectives

The objectives of the exercise are to: (1) understand and analyse a key passage in a historical text; (2) pick out key words from the passage in question.

Resources required

- [ ] Piece of text to analyse
- [ ] Post-It notes (stickers)
- [ ] Coloured marker pens
- [ ] A classroom wall

Breakdown of method in action

Time needed	Phase of activity
5 mins	Teacher introduces session and topic for debate.
10 mins	In mini-groups, pupils familiarise themselves with the piece of text that is under the spotlight. They are asked to identify, and then pick out, two key words from the passage. Then they must write up their words on stickers (one per sticker – in big lettering).
20 mins	Individuals, in turn, are invited to come to the wall and stick up their Post-It notes. The groups do this one at a time: each time a different person must get up, place a sticker on the wall, and explain why he or she chose the word they did. As they do this, they must show great awareness of the stickers that the other groups have put up – creating suitable clusters of similar words when and where appropriate.

10 mins	Teacher chairs a big-group plenary on the exercise – and what has emerged from the class's exploration of the text.

(Total time needed = 45 minutes)

Good exemplars

1 *Italian Unification*

Source *Speech of Victor Emanuel II, King of Italy (1861)*

> Free, and nearly entirely united, the opinion of civilized nations is favorable to us; the just and liberal principles, now prevailing in the councils of Europe, are favorable to us. Italy herself, too, will become a guarantee of order and peace, and will once more be an efficacious instrument of universal civilization ... These facts have inspired the nation with great confidence in its own destinies. I take pleasure in manifesting to the first Parliament of Italy the joy I feel ... as king and soldier.

Which key words would a group pick out?

Possibly:

CIVILISED and DESTINIES

2 *Modern China*

Source *The Atomic Bomb, Statement of the Government of the People's Republic of China (16 October 1964)*

> China exploded an atomic bomb at 15.00 hours on October 16, 1964, thereby successfully carrying out its first nuclear test. This is a major achievement of the Chinese people in their struggle to strengthen their national defence and oppose the US imperialist policy of nuclear blackmail and nuclear threats. To defend oneself is the inalienable right of every sovereign state. To safeguard world peace is the common task of all peace-loving countries. China cannot remain idle in the face of the ever increasing nuclear threats from the United States. China is conducting nuclear tests and developing nuclear weapons under compulsion. The Chinese Government has consistently

advocated the complete prohibition and thorough destruction of nuclear weapons. If this had been achieved, China need not have developed nuclear weapons. But our proposal has met with stubborn resistance from the US imperialists.

Which key words would a group pick out?

Possibly:

ACHIEVEMENT and RESISTANCE

3 Revolutions of 1848

Source   *Guizot speech (15 February 1842)*

I am, for my part, a decided enemy of universal suffrage. I look upon it as the ruin of democracy and liberty. If I needed proof I would have it under my very eyes; I will not elucidate. However, I should permit myself to say, with all the respect I have for a great country and a great government, that the inner danger, the social danger by which the United States appears menaced is due especially to universal suffrage; it is that which makes them run the risk of seeing their real liberties, the liberties of everybody, compromised, as well as the inner order of their society . . .

Which key words would a group pick out?

Possibly:

RUIN and ORDER

Learning outcomes

Following the activity, learners will be able to: (1) identify the most poignant or important words in a text; (2) review the main themes in a passage; (3) establish connections between words and themes chosen by themselves and other group members.

Summary

Merits?

☐ The 'practical task' element focuses pupils' minds and provokes genuine discussion.

☐ Encourages individuals to take responsibility for their own ideas.

☐ The wall with notes is the classroom focus – not the teacher.

☐ The 'clusters' are extremely interesting – and promote spontaneous discussion (e.g. 'Why has every group picked out that specific word?' 'Where should I put this word?').

☐ Gets pupils moving round the classroom.

Possible problems?

☐ Post-It notes: the perception that somehow anything new or different or involving new 'tools' is not a proper learning technique.

☐ Confusion about the notion of 'clusters'.

Finetuning?

☐ Ask pupils to pick out less obvious words – to avoid repetition.

☐ The teacher, or perhaps even a member of the class, concludes the session by rearranging the stickers in line with their own views about the topic under discussion.

Further reading

J. Byrom, 'Working with Sources', *Teaching History*, May 1998.

G. Howells, 'Gladstone Spiritual or Gladstone Material? A Rationale for using Documents at AS and A2', *Teaching History*, August 2000.

H. Le Cocq, 'Beyond Bias: Making Source Evaluation Meaningful to Year 7', *Teaching History*, May 2000.

M. Pearce, 'Sources for Courses: On Varying Types of Source', *Teaching History*, July, 1988.

T. McAleavy, 'The Use of Sources in History', *Teaching History*, May 1998.

Review

Within the historical community, the interpretation of primary texts can sometimes be problematic. This is because there are often different ways of interpreting the same text. The ten alternative activities explained and considered in this chapter can aid our attempts at historical enquiry. They actively promote a more discriminating awareness of the way in which history is taught and understood. This in turn leads on to an immediate and empathetic identification with the historical topic being studied.

This does not mean that the rigour of historical enquiry is lost – far from it. In the ten practical activities presented in this chapter, the intention has been to convey the essence of history as an academic subject and to promote further interest and research. Historical exploration is often quite personal; the obvious enjoyment and satisfaction that we have witnessed in experimenting with the ten activities has convinced us of the merits of a more hands-on approach to our subject. Young people can make history 'their own' by viewing the larger picture and by exploring possibilities and potential.

SUMMARY

The authors of this book hope that any teachers who use it will discover a selection of teaching methods to suit their particular needs and circumstances. In the four main areas – Visuals, Numerical Data, Concepts and Primary Texts – we hope that we have advanced a workable series of practical ideas for classroom use. Obviously a teacher planning to employ a technique introduced in the book needs to use his or her discretion in the way that the activity is put into operation and the way that it is managed, but we hope that we have set out the necessary general guidelines.

But, this book is just a start. If imaginative, practical classroom ideas can be used to good effect in our four chosen spheres, they can also, surely, be employed in others. In this sense, there is clearly room for a sequel – that would deal with other 'problematic' teaching and learning areas. For the moment though, our hope is that this book becomes, more than anything else, a useful, provocative and stimulating resource for teachers.

BIBLIOGRAPHY

A.E. Adams (ed.), *The Russian Revolution and Bolshevik Victory*, Boston, Heath, 1960.

J. Arch Getty and R.T. Manning, *Stalinist Terror*, Cambridge, CUP, 1994.

J-J. Becker, *The Great War and the French People*, Oxford, Berg, 1993.

M. Broszat, *The Hitler State*, London, Longman, 1981.

C. Brown and P. Mooney, *Cold War to Détente*, London, Heinemann, 1978.

C. Culpin, *Discovering the Past: Y7 Contrasts and Connections*, London, John Murray, 1991.

R. Dahl, *Polyarchy: Participation and Opposition*, New Haven, Yale University Press, 1971.

Division of History Resource Pack, University of Huddersfield.

Extended Writing in Key Stage 3 History, London, School Curriculum and Assessment Authority, 1997.

T. Fiehn, *Russia and the USSR 1905–1941: A Study in Depth*, London, John Murray, 1996.

C. Fischer, *The Rise of the Nazis*, Manchester, MUP, 1995.

J. Foxe, *Foxe's Book of Martyrs*, London, Word, 2000.

T. Franck, *The Power of Legitimacy among Nations*, New York, OUP, 1990.

P. Frederick, 'Motivating Students by Active Learning in the History Classroom', *Perspectives*, Oct 1993.

M.A.R. Graves, *The Tudor Parliaments*, London, Longman, 1995.

Hamer, *Life and Work in 19th Century Britain*, London, Heinemann, 1995.

G. Hardach, *The First World War*, London, Penguin, 1987.

D. Heater, *Case Studies in Twentieth Century World History*, London, Longman, 1988.

Holocaust Memorial Day, *Remembering Genocides: Lessons for the Future* (Education Pack), 2000.

N. Kelly, R. Rees and P. Shuter, *Living Through History: Medieval Realms*, London, Heinemann, 1997.

D. Kolb, *The Process of Experiential Learning*, New Jersey, Prentice-Hall, 1984.

G. Lacey and K. Shephard, *Germany 1918–1945: A Study in Depth*, London, John Murray, 1997.

R. Maples, *Modern British and European History*, London, Letts, 1985.

J. Martell, *A History of Britain from 1867*, London, Nelson, 1988.

K.O. Morgan (ed.), *The Oxford History of Britain*, Oxford, OUP, 1991.

J. Noakes and G. Pridham, *Nazism 1919–1945 Vol. I: The Rise to Power 1919–1934*, Exeter, University of Exeter Press, 1991.

G. Petty, *Teaching Today: A Practical Guide*, Cheltenham, Stanley Thornes, 1993.

J.A.G. Roberts, *Modern China: An Illustrated History*, Stroud, Sutton, 2000.

G. Salvemini, *The Origins of Fascism in Italy*, New York, Harper & Row, 1961.

Schools History Project, *Discovering the Past*, London, John Murray, 1991.

C. Shephard and B. Brown, *Britain 1750–1900*, London, John Murray, 1997.

J. Simkin, *National Curriculum History: Medieval Realms Resource Book*, Brighton, Spartacus Educational, 1991.

A. Smith, *Accelerated Learning in Practice*, Stafford, Network Educational Press, 1998.

J. Traynor and I. Dawson, *The Struggle for Peace 1918–1989*, London, Nelson, 1997.

J. Watson, *Success in Twentieth Century World Affairs*, London, John Murray, 1974.

A. Williams, *The English and the Norman Conquest*, Woodbridge, Boydell, 1997.

T. Wright, *Educational Policy Studies*, University of Alberta, <http://www.ualberta,ca/~tswright>.

Internet sites

<http://landow.stg.brown.edu/victorian/history/chartism7.html>

<http://www.fordham.edu/halsall/mod/modsbook46.html> (The Internet Modern History Sourcebook).

INDEX

Page numbers in *italics* indicate figures and tables.